ICT Changing Education

7 [
BC

Information and Communications Technology (ICT) is changing the face of education. In this timely and accessible book, Chris Abbott examines the process by which ICT, and in particular its role in relation to literacy, has become central to national educational policies.

The author traces the history of computer use in schools and examines the concept of virtual learning communities using case studies involving learners, parents and educationalists. The role of the Internet is considered along with the differing national policies on its adoption and on developing online content. *ICT: Changing Education* reveals the development of open and flexible learning outside school as the next stage of ICT's involvement with education.

Chris Abbott is a Lecturer in Education at King's College, University of London. His teaching and research relates to ICT, literacy and special educational needs, and the use of the Internet by young people. He has taught in special and mainstream schools and was Director of the Inner London Educational Computing Centre.

ICT: Changing Education

London: Routledge Farmer,   0750709502

Master Classes in Education Series
Series Editors: John Head, School of Education,
King's College, University of London and
Ruth Merttens, School of Education, University of
North London

ICT: Changing Education

Chris Abbott

London and New York

First published 2001 by RoutledgeFalmer
11 New Fetter Lane, London EC4P 4EE

Simultaneously published in the USA and Canada
by RoutledgeFalmer
29 West 35th Street, New York, NY 10001

RoutledgeFalmer is an imprint of the Taylor & Francis Group

Typeset in Sabon by Taylor & Francis Books Ltd
Printed and bound in Great Britain by TJ International Ltd, Padstow,
Cornwall

British Library Cataloguing in Publication Data
A catalogue record for this book is available from the British Library

Library of Congress Cataloging in Publication Data
Abbott, Chris, 1951 –
ICT: changing education / Chris Abbott.
p. cm. – (Master classes in education series)
Includes bibliographical references and index.
1. Computer-assisted instruction – Social aspects. 2. Internet
(Computer network) in education – Social aspects. 3. Educational
technology – History. I. Title.
II. Series.
LB1028.5 .A215 2000
371.33'09 – dc21
                                        00–042486

ISBN 0–7507–0951–0 (hbk)
ISBN 0–7507–0950–2 (pbk)

This book is dedicated to my parents, Barbara and Stanley Abbott, without whose support and dedication I would not have received the education which enabled me to write it.

Contents

Contents

Tables

Series Editors' Preface

It has become a feature of our times that an initial qualification is no longer seen to be adequate for life-long work within a profession and that programmes of professional development are needed. Nowhere is the need more clear than with respect to education, where changes in the national schooling and assessment system, combined with changes in the social and economic context, have transformed our professional lives.

The series, *Master Classes in Education*, is intended to address the needs of professional development, essentially at the level of taught masters degrees. Although aimed primarily at teachers and lecturers, it is envisaged that the books will appeal to a wider readership, including those involved in professional educational management, health promotion and youth work. For some, the texts will serve to update their knowledge. For others, they may facilitate career reorientation by introducing, in an accessible form, new areas of expertise or knowledge.

The books are overtly pedagogical, providing a clear track through the topic by means of which it is possible to gain a sound grasp of the whole field. Each book familiarises the reader with the vocabulary and the terms of discussion, and provides a concise overview of recent research and current debates in the area. While it is obviously not possible to deal with every aspect in depth, a professional who has read the book should be able to feel confident that they have covered the major areas of content, and discussed the different issues at stake. The books are also intended to convey a sense of the future direction of the subject and its points of growth or change.

In each subject area the reader is introduced to different perspectives and to a variety of readings of the subject under consideration. Some of the readings may conflict, others may be compatible but distant. Different perspectives may well give rise to different lexicons and different bibliographies, and the reader is always alerted to these differences. The variety of frameworks within which each topic can be construed is then a further source of reflective analysis.

The authors in this series have been carefully selected. Each person is an experienced professional, who has worked in that area of education as a practitioner and also addressed the subject as a researcher and theoretician. Drawing upon both pragmatic and the theoretical aspects of their experience, they are able to take a reflective view while preserving a sense of what occurs, and what is possible, at the level of practice.

ICT: Changing Education

Over the decades we have become used to claims that new technologies, including the introduction of teaching machines and the widespread use of television in schools, would revolutionise school practices. It has sometimes been suggested that within a finite time teachers would largely become unnecessary as the new technology takes over. In practice most of these developments have proved to offer no more than a possible tool to help teachers perform their traditional tasks.

It is now abundantly clear that the development of information and communication technologies is very different. Schooling and teaching will be forced to change in a variety of ways. At one level we now have to teach computer skills, not least because career prospects for our students may be dependent on the possession of such skills. Second, we have to prepare pupils for a society in which many traditional aspects of living have been transformed, aspects which include retailing, banking and communication by means such as e-mail.

There is no sign of this immense technological and social revolution slowing down. Computers are becoming ever more sophisticated. Just as in the past main-frame machines were largely replaced by PCs so even the newer systems, such as the Internet, are in turn threatened by yet newer developments, such as communicating via television systems.

Young children seem to take most of these technologies within their stride but as educationalists, we face the twofold task of keeping ourselves up to date and also anticipating the forms of future schooling.

Chris Abbott is the ideal person to guide us through this jungle. He combines a high level of technical knowledge with a deep commitment to humanistic values. A former teacher of English, he avoids unnecessary jargon and includes among his interests the creation of virtual communities among the young who through physical or mental handicap may find it difficult to socialise by other means.

As the former director of ILECC he has lived through and participated in the changes in recent decades, and he uses a historical approach to help us locate and understand the different aspects of ICT provision.

We confidently believe that this book will become **the** key text on ICT and education.

John Head
Ruth Merttens
Series Editors

Acknowledgements

I would like to thank John Head for his support and encouragement throughout the writing of this book; Linda Spear, Nic Lawrence, Diana Forster, Les Squirrel and Peter Andrews for contributing information; my ICT colleagues at King's College London, Barry Blakeley, Margaret Cox, David Squires, Deryn Watson, Lee Andrews and Jean Seechurn for their advice; the colleagues with whom I have worked at ILECC and within NAACE; international colleagues, especially Raymond Morel, Stanislav Zelenda, Miroslava Cernochova, Zdena Lustigova, Andrea Karpathi, Hilding Sponberg, Joop van Schie, Brigitta Gothberg and Caterina Brun; the special school teachers who have taught me so much, especially David Nicholls; my pupils, particularly Robert Caldecott who first showed me what computers were capable of; David Noble and colleagues in the DfEE; and my wife, Hazel Abbott, for reminding me that it is what happens in classrooms that really matters.

Tables 1-5 are reproduced by kind permission of the DfEE. Tables 6-9 are reproduced by kind permission of Dominic Savage, BESA.

Introduction

This book is not an attempt to predict the future, and neither is it a comprehensive history of the use of computers in schools. Either of those tasks, the one foolhardy and the other daunting, would require a much greater number of words, a different author and probably a different readership. What this book does aim to do is to select from the history of technology in education, and particularly from the twenty years during which computers have become significant, in order to understand the present and to consider possible future developments. It draws in particular on some writing by advocates of alternatives to schooling, such as Ivan Illich, as well as some of those who have written on this area within an ICT framework, such as Seymour Papert. I am also indebted to those commentators, such as Sherry Turkle and Julian Sefton-Green, who have written about young people, computers and the Internet.

Chapter 1, 'ICT and literacy', begins by examining this central issue and considers the ways in which notions of literacy are changing as a result of the use of Information and Communications Technology (ICT). Literacy and its acquisition is a central focus for schooling. Much of the political dialogue around ICT, and around earlier technologies, has related to claims for advances it may produce in the acquisition of literacy. Previous alliances of technology and literacy are mentioned and some of the early claims made for computers are considered. Definitions of literacy have expanded to recognise the diversity of literary transmission devices and genres, and the concepts of multiple literacies and multimedia texts that have become prevalent are discussed.

Chapter 2, 'Virtual communities', looks at the way in which ICT is changing communities and creating new and often virtual groupings. These virtual communities are examined through their manifestation as Webrings, Netrings and other online metaphors. Young people and their online identities are considered, as are the multiple identities of the online fictional world. Geographical separation, reduced by previous technologies such as short-wave radio and the telephone, is becoming ever more marginalised and made less relevant by moves towards virtual communities, in which shared ideology is more important than occupation of the same physical space. Notions of publishing and its effect on education are discussed, especially in the light of the possibilities offered by online versions of this activity, and as publishing becomes an activity available to all rather than one open only to a privileged or informed elite.

The extent to which ICT is changing the purpose of school is considered in Chapter 3, 'Changing schools', as is the movement of educational technology from its traditional base, the school, towards the home environment. The role of Information Technology (IT) as a subject in school is discussed, as well as the change to a focus on the cross-curricular use of ICT and the effects this has produced. The movement towards more open and flexible learning is considered in the light of an examination of the history of support for computer use in English schools, and the political imperatives that have driven this. The UK National Curriculum and its effect on the development of ICT as a subject is a focus for the later part of the chapter.

Chapter 4, 'Learning, computers and social interaction', develops the argument concerning the way in which education is being changed by ICT, and concentrates on social interaction between learners. This section is illustrated by a case study of a young person who has learned his professional IT skills in this way. Links between educational theory and the use of ICT are made, and the notion of post-geographical learning is proposed: learning, that is, which takes place through the online social interaction of groups whose members may not reside in physical proximity. A discussion of home-schooling indicates the extent to which the steady development of this phenomenon has been linked to ICT use and availability.

A range of solutions is considered in Chapter 5, 'Educational responses to technology', from the teaching machines of the 1960s to the multimedia-connected PC of the present day. Key developments in educational software, from the early drill-and-practice programs and programmed learning to multimedia authoring, are contrasted with concepts such as Integrated Learning Systems. A major focus here is the dichotomy between the computer as teaching machine and the computer as tool or support, and also considered are the 'machine wars' between different operating systems which bedevilled much of ICT progress in education until the mid-1990s. A case study of the software provided to primary schools in one UK education authority is used to indicate the assumptions made and the beliefs held at the time that computers first entered primary schools. Contrasts are drawn between much early behaviourist software and exceptional programs such as Developing Tray and Logo.

There have been dissenting voices throughout the development of the use of ICT in education. In Chapter 6, 'The rise of the Internet and the race to connect', some of these voices are heard, both in relation to the specific role of ICT in the classroom, and in connection with the all-pervasive nature of ICT use today. Apocalyptic predictions of the end of the book are contrasted with the superficial hype associated with the image of ICT-based education proposed in the popular press and promoted through computer-related advertising. The chapter deals also with the false dawns and dubious claims which have characterised much of the history of ICT in education. Learning systems, the humble BBC computer and the Internet in its earlier modem-based incarnation are examples of technology for which great claims have been made. The international race to connect is considered here too, with the UK vying with other nations to be the first to link all schools to the Internet, to be a centre of excellence for ICT-related products, and to establish an education system which is technologically advanced. UK developments are considered alongside those of a number of other countries and a comparison is made between developments in some of these countries and the policy statements behind them.

Chapter 7, 'Towards a new understanding of ICT and schools', draws together this range of change and development in order to propose a new understanding of the potential and limitations of ICT within a changing educational system. The concept of target-setting, especially with the European sector, forms a useful basis for comparison. A particular focus is on the major challenges facing the secondary education sector, the sector most likely to see major change in the light of technological advances. Current developments in this area are considered as indications of possible ways forward, and the final section of the chapter considers what school might become in the relatively near future.

As has been stated, this is not intended to be a work of prediction or futurology. It does not seek to persuade others to use ICT; the intention is simply to put before the reader a range of events that have happened, practices that have developed and trends that can be traced. As it has been written by an English teacher who became involved with computers only after teaching without them for fifteen years, it does claim to be the product of someone whose fascination for the subject of ICT in education has at all times been tempered by his pragmatic recognition of what is possible within classrooms. That fascination, however, continues to develop; and what is possible has grown beyond most people's expectation.

1   ICT and Literacy

The suggestion that there might come a day when schools no longer exist
elicits strong responses from many people. There are many obstacles to
thinking clearly about a world without schools. Some are highly personal.
Most of us spent a larger fraction of our lives going to school than we care
to think about. ... The concept of a world without school is highly disso-
nant with our experiences of our own lives. Other obstacles are more
conceptual. One cannot define such a world negatively, that is by simply
removing school and putting nothing in its place. Doing so leaves a thought
vacuum that the mind has to fill one way or another, often with vague but
scary images of children 'running wild', 'drugging themselves' or 'making
life impossible for their parents'. Thinking seriously about a world without
school calls for elaborated models of the non-school activities in which
children would engage.

(Papert, 1993: 178)

One of the aims of this book is to begin to develop some suitable models
of what school is becoming at the beginning of a new century. It is written
from a belief that we are no longer faced with a decision as to whether
schools should change, but with the reality that our concepts of school,
learning and education have developed and fragmented to such an extent
that the identification of schooling with a 100-year-old building full of
teenagers who do not want to be there is no longer seen as either appropriate or defensible by many. It is the central thesis of this book that, to a
large extent, it is the increased availability of Information and
Communication Technologies (ICT) that has brought about this change of
thinking.

What has become recognised ever more widely since Papert wrote the
passage above is that ICT is already changing society, and therefore education, even if schools do continue. The impact of change is not only
technological but also social. The Internet is already changing practices in
banking and shopping and in the creation of virtual communities, and any
vision of the future of education has to recognise new methods of
accessing information and new ways of relating to others. We begin this

4

book as we will end it, by considering the fulcrum on which the intersection of ICT and schooling rests: the teacher.

ICT and Literacy: The Technologically Literate Teacher

> Books will soon be obsolete in the schools. Scholars will soon be instructed through the eye. It is possible to teach every branch of human knowledge with the motion picture. Our school system will be completely changed in ten years.
>
> (*New York Dramatic Mirror*, 1913, quoted in Saettler, 1968: 98)

Entering the teaching profession in the early 1970s, as I did, involved grappling with the technology of the day. The epidiascope, a Heath Robinson-like assemblage of lights and mirrors, had enthralled me as a 1950s primary pupil. It had the ability, for example, to project on to a large screen images of constellations that totally absorbed me and my fellow New Elizabethans. By the time I began teaching such wonderful devices were no longer available, and the teaching machines that made a brief appearance at my grammar school in the 1960s, and will be considered when we look at the history of programmed learning, had long been consigned to a cupboard.

It was the Banda, the spirit copier, which formed for teachers in that period the height of technological aspiration. Mysterious and multi-sensory, the Banda is remembered by older generations of teachers as much for its smell and its ability to print purple marks on any inappropriate but light-coloured surface as it is for its most important facility: the ability it gave to teachers to make multiple copies of a printed text or even image. After a century or more of the textbook in ascendancy, the Banda was the advance party for the future pairing of computer and photocopier, which would transform teacherly practice through access to these technologies.

There were other devices available to the literacy teacher of the 1970s, of course: having developed an early interest in the teaching of reading I soon experimented with the Language Master, which provided speech feedback when flash cards were passed through it. These cards, usually flash cards containing single words, had a magnetic strip on the reverse which carried a speech recording. This was an early example of a technology simply modelling an existing practice – the use of flash cards in the teaching of reading – and adding some technological facility to the resource. Like the talking book software of the 1980s, the fundamental principle was that technology should add to rather than change practice. This would become an unsupportable stance to take in the light of later conflicting evidence.

The Ricoh Synchrofax too, sometimes known as the Audio Page, offered an early opportunity to attempt a fusion of text and spoken language, which only became fully usable years later, after the advent of speech cards in computers with sufficient memory. An A4 card was completely covered in magnetic material on one side, enabling several sentences of audio to be recorded and then played back while viewing the text or image that had been fixed to the reverse. Both devices were complex to use and required attendance at in-service training courses from teachers who wished to use them; and within a few years both had all but disappeared as the computer offered the same facilities and much more.

Current multimedia software and Internet access bring a vast array of image-based information into the classroom. Before becoming available via the computer, this kind of information was found in the school library and, on occasions, through the use of 16mm film, filmstrips and, later, videotape and then cassette. For a teacher to become proficient in the use of a 16mm film projector often required attendance at a whole series of training sessions, and even the humble filmstrip seemed to be destined to be inserted upside down and back-to-front before the correct orientation could be found. Bringing film into the classroom was often seen then as a revolutionary or even puzzling practice; was it not the case, it was suggested, that 'watching a film is a solitary experience. ... We go out to a movie, to a special building or room constructed for that purpose alone' (Ruth, 1977: 110). It is interesting to note that the same article looks forward quite perceptively to the advent of cable and satellite television but that in the whole of a lengthy article on new non-print media there is no mention of the computer. Until relatively recent times, computers were seen as resolutely text-based. Even in 1985, a major volume dealing with the teaching of literacy contained the index entry 'Computers, see Word Processing' (White, 1985).

It is now routine to see moving images on television and computer screens in classrooms, but it is easy to forget that this is a relatively recent development. Twenty years ago the use of video would be likely to involve moving the whole class to a viewing room, with early tape-based video players being both expensive and difficult to operate. In most secondary schools it was necessary to book a technician or Media Resources Officer to operate the videotape player, with the clear message being that the operation of technology was a specialised activity beyond the skills that could be expected of a teacher. The technological skills expected of a teacher in the present day, by contrast, are probably in excess of those possessed by the resources technicians of that earlier era.

It was in the area of reprographics that technology was just beginning, in the 1970s, to change teacher practice, and was sowing the seeds of the process which is now accelerating. First the spirit copier, then the ink duplicator and finally and most crucially the photocopier changed for good the relationship between teacher, text and technology.

By 1994 in the United States the *Telecommunications Policy Review* (11 June 1994: 1) was confidently stating that 84 per cent of American teachers considered only one type of technology to be absolutely essential: a photocopier with an adequate paper supply. Photocopiers became part of teacherly practice in a way that computers are only just beginning to approach. It has been suggested (Marcus, 1993) that we move through two stages in our embrace of new technology, with the first stage characterised by ambivalence about the extra possibilities offered and only the later stage leading to what has been called the 'dawning of irreversible change' (Midani, 1986).

Irreversible change is certainly an apt summary of the effect of the photocopier on teacher practice. Where once the textbook ruled supreme, it is now routine for teachers to select from a much wider range of resources; to change those resources from year to year or from lesson to lesson, and to differentiate the learning activities they give to pupils in their care. ICT has the potential to cause irreversible change in classrooms and schools, and has sometimes done so already; at other sites the machines simply wait in readiness like the characters in a science-fiction story, later to fulfil their potential.

Great claims have been made for the importance of the PC: the invention of the digital computer has even been described as 'the single most revolutionary moment in the history of representation since the emergence of language' (Dibbell, 1998: 56). Whether that moment was or was not revolutionary for the way in which society educates its young is the topic of this book, and efforts will be made to suggest that such a revolution is approaching, if not yet quite upon us.

Computers and Changing Literacy

> Future courses may not be examined by testing the limits of an individual's memory but instead may challenge a student's strategies for obtaining information quickly, for ordering it into a logical sequence, for arriving at conclusions from given facts and for accurate and rapid problem solving.
>
> (Hills, 1980: 45)

In his far-sighted book dealing with the future of the printed word, Hills raises many of the issues to be discussed here. Even in 1980 he foresaw the changes which would have to come for traditional secondary education. In particular, he noted 'a possible trend away from the formal educational setting – a building specifically set aside for the purposes of education where teachers teach and students learn – towards a more home-based educational system' (Hills, 1980: 41). We will return to this concept, now a very prevalent one, in the final chapter.

It is its ability to provide and retrieve information, together with its potential as a communicative tool, rather than as a teacher substitute, that is the basis for claims that the computer will change schooling irrevocably. As has been described elsewhere (Gates, 1999), the idea of a tool that enables one to access information is not new, and can be traced back to Dr Vannervar Bush's Memex machine, which he described in 1945. Bush's idea was to design a storage system which would enable the retrieval of items but also their linkage to other data stored in the same system, a process he called 'associative indexing'. Although his methodology now looks impossibly cumbersome, Bush did, as Gates acknowledges, predict 'the multimedia PC connected to the Web ... [and] the equivalent of Internet search engines' (Gates, 1999: 165).

Many of today's teachers grew up in a pre-computer world, and may even have moved through the handwriting technologies of pencil, then nib pen, ballpoint and fountain pen. They may well remember the excitement that accompanied the invention of the ink cartridge, solving as it did the blotting and spillage problems of thousands of clumsy children – and of quite a few teachers. Many adults will remember their first personal meeting with the world of printing, which was for many in the UK a John Bull printing set. This popular birthday present of the middle years of the twentieth century consisted of a large number of small rubber printing letters together with an ink pad and some slotted wooden letter block holders. The first task, in those far-off days when sharp objects were sometimes permitted in infant hands, was to separate all the letters with a razor blade. This done, the gleeful recipient could set about printing with abandon, although always irritated by the inevitable shortage of particular much-needed letters: there were never enough Es.

The next stage for many was the acquisition of a typewriter, a complex piece of writing technology that has many links with the computer, not least the similarity between the keyboards used by both as input devices. Typewriters existed for well over a hundred years but are no longer manufactured anywhere in the world. Reconditioned models are still produced in India, coincidentally the country popularly supposed to have the fastest growing number of computer users. It appears to be a myth that the keyboard layout of a typewriter is designed to slow down users and therefore avoid clashing levers. Despite the claims of the advocates of speech recognition, however, this layout and the various national variants of it look likely to live on for many years through their adoption as computer keyboards.

The typewriter has been a key technological device for access to information; used to type underground newspapers in repressive states, it is also seen on the streets of many developing countries, where the literate but poor can earn a living by typing letters for others without the appropriate skills. The combination of typewriter and photocopier – or duplicator – can be a threatening one to totalitarian states, and photocopiers in particular are sometimes legally accessible only to those who are trusted by the state to conform.

These issues of access to print and the effect this has on society have been the subject of much interest (Eisenstein, 1983; Spender, 1995), with suggestions that the establishment, and in particular the established church, felt greatly threatened by the growing ability to read of wider sections of society. Although they deal with similar developments, Eisenstein and Spender approach the issue from different perspectives. Spender emphasises those aspects of the post-printing period which aimed to preserve old ways rather than to capitalise on new possibilities, whereas Eisenstein seeks to explain and illuminate a period she sees as one of great change, energy and renewal. Spender, writing more than ten years after Eisenstein, deals at length with the contemporary literary artefact which is the World Wide Web homepage, another development in mass literacy which has also been attacked and denigrated by those who, in some cases, stand to lose their previously privileged literacy status. Her remarks on the attitude of the established church could also be applied to much of the reaction to the availability of online publication.

> According to the Church, the new custom of allowing everyone to go off and read in isolation and to develop opinions of their own was a recipe for anarchy and disaster. ... The members of the establishment ... were trying to hang on to their own skills ... they didn't want changes which marginalised them and left them feeling worthless and useless. That is why they kept insisting that the old ways were the only ways and that the new should be fiercely resisted.
>
> (Spender, 1995: 8)

Spender also attributes much of what she sees as the 'dismay and distress at the passing of the print era' as being directly related to the way in which the rise of computer technology has sounded the death knell for the 'patriarchal presence that has been encoded in communication' (Spender, 1995: 10).

By the end of the twentieth century it was no longer possible to view literacy as based on the word or even on the word-based text. Literacy today is essentially multimedia, composed of an amalgam of words, pictures, sounds and the moving image. Lanham was among the first to deal with the shift in literacy and in terms of what he described as the icon/alphabet ratio (Lanham, 1994), the process by which images have become part of, rather than ancillary to, texts. Understanding of this process was taken much further by others, especially Kress, who has focused on visual literacy in much of his writing (Kress, 1982, 1993; Kress and Van Leeuwen, 1996). In *The Grammar of Visual Design* (1996), written with Van Leeuven, Kress attempts to describe this development in linguistic terms.

Sharples' analysis of writing as an act of creative design offers an account of the mental, physical and social aspects of writing, which acknowledges the central role of the newer computer-based technologies in affecting and forming literacy practices and processes. He suggests that technology is changing the very nature of writing, and that the intelligent computer, the 'weaver of texts and teller of tales' (Sharples, 1999: 205) may be the eventual outcome of the move to automation within literacy. Alongside growing acceptance of the concept of virtual literacy came the allied idea of an identifiable and desired information literacy (Loveless and Longman, 1998) and the implications of this for teachers.

Kress and others in the New London Group (NLG) produced an influential paper (New London Group, 1996) at a time when the Internet, in particular, was first attaining its ascendancy in the discussion of computer-related literacy practices. The paper deals with what it sees as the changing social environment facing students and teachers, and calls for a much wider view of literacy than has previously been current. The members of the NLG take this stance in the expectation that such an understanding will enable two goals to be achieved: access for students to the changing ways in which work, power and community are described, and assistance for students who wish to get involved with these changes so that they can control and plan their own future social and working lives.

The NLG develop in their paper the notion of multi-literacies, which suggests that literacy is not only changing but fragmenting into a series of different but allied literacies. Some members of the group have written elsewhere (Kress, 1996a) on this topic and suggested (Kress, 1996b) the concept of dynamic representational resources, a term developed from Critical Discourse Analysis and a more inclusive and cohesive take on the issue. In his response to the NLG paper, Street (1996) contrasts the notion of multi-literacies with what he describes as multiple literacies. In his 1996 address and in later writing (Street, 1998, 1999), Street argues that the multi-literacies approach might be located in an understanding of the historical context within which literacy, and computer technology, has developed. He considers three models of literacy: the Autonomous model, Critical Literacy and New Literacy Studies; and then argues that although multi-literacies need not be located within one of these areas, the NLG are at least under an obligation to take account of these positions on literacy.

Street sees the autonomous model of literacy as rooted in technological determinism, and it is therefore tempting to see this as the conceptual model most suited to this study. However, as will be shown in a later chapter, computer-mediated learning and literacy are essentially the products of social interaction. Street's linking of the Critical Literacy approach with post-modernism and a recognition of irrevocable change also suggests an apparent link with literacies which are themselves linked to newer technologies. New Literacy Studies, on the other hand, is characterised by Street as being centrally involved with communication and social relationships; again central facets of online and computer-mediated literacy. Street's concept of literacy practices is also highly relevant to the approach taken here to ICT in education, and it is within the New Literacy Studies approach that the current volume would seek to be placed.

Chapter Summary

- ICT is changing our notion of what schooling consists of and how it should be delivered.
- Notions of literacy have been changed and developed as a result of ICT, and literacy is central to most definitions of education.
- ICT in the classroom can be seen as part of a continuum dealing with the use of previous forms of instructional technology.
- Aspects of ICT use offer access to information or the means of publication which may prove threatening to historically privileged individuals or states.
- ICT is becoming less related to the word-based text and is now essentially multimedia, involving sound, pictures and the moving image.

Bibliography

Dibbell, J. (1998). *My Tiny Life: Crime and Passion in a Virtual World*. London: Fourth Estate.

Eisenstein, E. (1983). *The Printing Revolution in Early Modern Europe*. Cambridge: Cambridge University Press.

Gates, B. (1999). *Business Using a Digital Nervous System*. London: Penguin.

Hills, P. (1980). The place of the printed word in teaching and learning. In P. Hills (ed.), *The Future of the Printed Word: The Impact and Implications of the New Communications Technology* (37–46). London: Frances Pinter.

Kress, G. (1982). *Learning to Write*. London: Routledge & Kegan Paul.

—— (1993). Against arbitrariness: the social production of the sign as a foundational issue in critical discourse analysis. *Discourse & Society*, 4(2), 169–91.

—— (1996a). Internationalisation and globalisation: rethinking a curriculum of communication. *Comparative Education*, 31 (2), 185–96.

—— (1996b). Representational resources and the production of subjectivity. In C. R. Caldas-Coulthard and M. Coulthard (eds), *Texts and Practices: Readings in Critical Discourse Analysis* (15–31). London: Routledge.

Kress, G. and Van Leeuwen, T. (1996). *Reading Images: The Grammar of Visual Design*. London: Routledge.

Lanham, R. (1994). *The Electronic Word: Democracy, Technology, and the Arts.* Chicago: University of Chicago Press.

Loveless, A. and Longman, D. (1998). Information literacy: innuendo or insight? *Education and Information Technologies*, 3, 27–40.

Marcus, S. (1993). Multimedia, hypermedia and the teaching of English. In M. Monteith (ed.), *Computers and Language*, (21–43). Oxford: Intellect Books.

Midani, A. (1986). A matter of perception. Featured address – EDUCOM '86, Pittsburgh, Pennsylvania.

New London Group (1996). A Pedagogy of Multiliteracies: Designing Social Futures. *Harvard Educational Review*, 66 (1), 60–92.

Papert, S. (1993). *Mindstorms: Children, Computers and Powerful Ideas* (2nd edn). New York: Basic Books.

Ruth, D. (1977). The Next Language Art: Views of Nonprint Media. In J. Squire (ed.), *The Teaching of English*. Chicago: University of Chicago Press.

Saettler, P. (1968). *A History of Instructional Technology*. New York: McGraw Hill.

Sharples, M. (1999). *How We Write*. London: Routledge.

Spender, D. (1995). *Nattering on the Net: Women, Power and Cyberspace.* Melbourne: Spinifex Press.

Street, B. (1996). Multiple literacies and multi-literacies. Paper presented at the Domains of Literacy, Institute of Education, London.

—— (1998). Literacy 'events' and literacy 'practices': theory and practice in the 'new literacy studies'. In M. Martin-Jones (ed.), *Multilingual Literacies: Comparative Perspectives on Research and Practice*. Amsterdam: John Benjamin's.

—— (1999). New literacies in theory and practice: what are the implications for language in education? *Linguistics and Education*, 10 (1), 1–24.

White, E. (1985). *Teaching and Assessing Writing*. San Francisco: Jossey-Bass.

2   Virtual Communities

> The age of the online pioneers will end soon, and the cyberspace settlers
> will come en-masse. ... Students and scientists are already there, artists
> have made significant inroads, librarians and educators have their own
> pioneers as well, and political activists of all stripes have just begun to
> discover the power of plugging a computer into a telephone.
>
> (Rheingold, 1996: 415)

For many observers, the words 'online' and 'community' do not easily sit
together: online life is seen as essentially alone and lacking in human
contact. To assess the activity in this way is to bring to a new environment
the values and measures of a previous one. Many users of the Internet see
themselves as part of communities that transcend and even replace some of
the day-to-day contact with other human beings which has been seen as
essential to community life.

In this chapter, an examination of the early attempts to develop virtual
communities is included in order to show that many of the current
concerns about online life have been noted for many years. Reference to
previous community-building activities with the telephone and, particularly, CB radio show that the urge to build community through technology
is not a new development. As online communities left the world of
dungeons, dragons and myths, they began to attract the attention of other
commentators, and the work of writers such as Howard Rheingold is
discussed in this context.

Business communities are changing too, as has been documented by Bill
Gates among others; and it is business in the form of Web-based commerce
that is responsible for artificial community devices such as Webrings and
the easy availability of Web homepage templates, both of them influential
developments for virtual groupings.

Virtual Communities before Computers

For almost the first hundred years of its existence, the telephone was mostly thought of as a dialogue tool for two people at a time. Although various listening-in devices became available quite quickly, these usually permitted others to listen but not to take part in discussions. Audio bridges developed the possibilities of telephony, enabling many-to-many conferencing calls to take place, as did some of the commercial chat services that developed in the 1980s and 1990s. These were later the focus of considerable concern, leading to greater regulation of access and moderation of content, a development that would be mirrored on the Internet a few years later. The anonymous groups of phone chatters on these systems were the forerunners of the much larger and more specialised groupings that would develop through the use of Internet Relay Chat (IRC) and Web-based chat programs.

Citizens' Band (CB) radio was a first indication of the desire that people have to form communities through communicative technology. Often used by people who already considered themselves members of a community, such as truck drivers or people living in remote areas, CB radio quickly developed a terminology and vocabulary of its own, very much as online chat systems were to do in later years. It is no surprise that CompuServe, one of the first major online services to penetrate the home market, called its first chat area the CB Forum. The beginning of online communities, however, can be traced back to two early Internet developments: the rapidly burgeoning newsgroups world and the rather more arcane area inhabited by the denizens of fictional electronic narratives. We need to examine both of these, but will consider first the general area of identity online.

Identity and Community

If a notion of self needs to be developed before a feeling of community can follow, then the writers who have seen fit to link the two could offer enlightenment to those seeking to understand this area. Foremost in an understanding of young people and the link between their use of computers and their sense of self is Shelley Turkle, who has written on this topic over a lengthy period (Turkle, 1984, 1996). It is Turkle's notion of the computer as linked to identity at adolescence that has informed previous writing on the topic (Abbott, 1999). It has been suggested that, at adolescence, young people have to make 'a series of self-defining choices to allow them to function as autonomous adults' (Head, 1997: 7). These choices are more commonly thought of as a facet of real life (RL), but they can equally well form part of online existence. When a young person chooses an image, a form of words or even a colour for his homepage, he (and in the past it has most often been a young male) is making a definite choice. By doing so, as has been shown (Abbott, 1999), he is at least in part doing so in order to present an image or identity of himself which accords with his hopes and wishes as to how the rest of the world will view him.

Psychological perspectives on adolescence (Head, 1997) merge here with ideas from the world of human–computer interaction (Turkle, 1984, 1996) to suggest that adolescence is a search for identity, and that at adolescence young people see computers as a means of establishing that identity. Turkle has characterised three stages in children's relationships with computers: metaphysical, mastery and, at adolescence, identity (Turkle, 1984: 9). If cyberspace technologies really do change who we think we are and how we relate to others (Cutler, 1996; Meyerowitz, 1985), then it is likely that there will be fundamental associated changes in notions of time, sense, space and place. Identity, we are told, is 'additive and growth continuous' (Lipton, 1996: 343) and we should expect to see two key patterns developing: multiple selves and fragmented identities.

As has been shown in my previous research (Abbott, 1999), and in the writings of others (Jones, 1997; Ludlow, 1996; Shields, 1996; Spender, 1995; Tapscott, 1998; Turkle, 1996), identity assumption is a major part of Internet play and practice. As such, it is a feature of unrestricted access for long periods of time; it is for this reason that much of the earlier research describes academics and students assuming elaborate and overtly literary identities in complex online games, for they were the only people to have such access for many years. Now that much larger numbers of young people have unlimited access, especially in the USA where the length of time spent online has never been related to increased costs, the spectrum of users assuming new identities is much wider and more diverse. In 1999, services in the UK began offering access via a free 0800 phone line in the evenings and at weekends, leading to the possibility of access free of time charges in the UK for the first time.

Even those social groups previously seen as disenfranchised from these facilities are beginning to get such access, especially with the arrival of television-based services such as WebTV in the USA and Europe. In mid-1999 it was reported that 50 per cent of the homes in the USA had Internet access (*San Jose Mercury News Online*, 11 April 1999) and that the gender imbalance of those online, at least in the USA, was no longer as extreme. According to a US Internet Council report (quoted in the *Washington Times*, 13 April 1999), in the USA 23 per cent of black people, 36 per cent of Hispanics and almost 50 per cent of women are now online. There are, of course, different definitions of being online, and there may still be issues of availability in households where everyone has an e-mail address but young male fingers seem to have privileged access to the available keyboards.

Turkle also sees differences between those young people for whom computers have become a way of life and those in the majority who integrate their computer experience into their wider-developing identities (Turkle, 1984: 139). The former group are much smaller in number, although they form the basis for the stereotype that causes so much concern among those who find the idea of many hours in front of a screen both unsettling and inappropriate. An alternative analysis of this activity (Sefton-Green, 1998) sees this not as an indication of introspection and passivity, but of engagement with a task and perseverance to its completion. The majority of young people who integrate computers into their everyday life use them as they use the trainers they wear, the music to which they listen or the aspirations they profess: as a means of developing an identity which is an amalgam of all of these aspects and more besides.

Online community has been a topic of interest to many writers over the last fifteen years, characterised by volumes such as *High Noon on the Electronic Frontier: Conceptual Issues in Cyberspace* (Ludlow, 1996). With chapter headings such as 'The clipper chip will block crime', 'Censorship and sysop liability' and 'How should we respond to exploratory hacking/cracking/phreaking?', it will be noted that this is not a book for those who are new to the subject under discussion. It starts beyond the point that many books have identified, and assumes value and interest in the subject matter before concentrating on detail and issues of current debate within the community. Some contributors do, however, deal with the wider picture, especially within the section on 'Self and community online'.

During the mid-1990s considerable interest was shown in the development of online communities (Jones, 1995, 1997; Rheingold, 1993, 1996; Shields, 1996), as has been made clear already when discussing the ideas and analyses put forward by these writers. Rheingold has been credited with having noted the development first (Rheingold, 1993), and others, such as Jones and Shields, have discussed community building as it exists in a variety of online and virtual environments. It has been suggested that such communities are ad hoc developments on the part of users, and that these phenomena represent unplanned responses to developing technologies and opportunities.

It is these developing communities which are discussed in *Internet Culture* (Porter, 1997) by a variety of authors and from various viewpoints. Porter's book opens with a section devoted to notions of community, which discusses the origins of the concept (Wilbur, 1997), the link with other forms of community engagement (Foster, 1997), the accepted rules of group behaviour (Tepper, 1997) and the link with the American literary tradition of the frontier (Healy, 1997).

Activity

Here is one set of definitions of virtual community; what might be the implications of this situation for the conventional school?

1   It is the experience of sharing with unseen others a space of communication.
2   For me it is the work of a few hours a day, carved up into minutes and carried on from before dawn until long after dark.
3   Virtual community is the illusion of a community where there are no real people and no real communication.
4   Virtual community has no necessary link to computers or to glossy high technologies.
5   Virtual community is the simulation of community, preferably with a large dose of tradition and very little mess.
6   Virtual community is people all over the world gathered around television sets to watch the Super Bowl or a World Cup match.
7   Virtual community is the new middle landscape, the garden in the machine, where democratic values can thrive in a sort of cyber-Jeffersonian renaissance.

(Summarised from Wilbur, 1997: 13–14)

To consider community is also to consider the construction of the self within that community. This has been seen as influenced by mediating technologies, whether these be the book, the computer or the Internet. Bolter's critique of the Cartesian definition of self (Bolter, 1996) suggests that this view was not created by print technology but was allowed to develop because of it. He suggests that in the Cartesian definition of self 'the visual and sensual aspects of human nature were subordinated to the faculty of reason'. He goes on to explain that this produced a situation where 'abstraction was privileged' and that part of the reason for the waning of this position is the effect of electronic technology:

> the new technology is playing a role in the redefinition of self. ... Electronic technology is helping to change the communicative balance between word and image in our media. ... It is the breakout of the visual that leads to new constructions of the self.

(Bolter, 1996: 111)

That this new technology is increasingly to be found in the home has led to discussion (Downes, 1996) of the extent to which this has implications for educationists. Others (Lanham, 1994), who have also analysed this changing balance between the word and the image, have sometimes argued that what is emerging is a post-modern definition of the self (Gergen, 1991). For Gergen, this post-modern self has been fragmented and changed by the effects of digital technologies.

Newsgroups

Newsgroups, sometimes collectively known as Usenet, were one of the first developments of the Internet. They capitalise on the vast number of users of the Internet and the ability it offers to search through information quickly by setting up many thousands of individual discussion groups related to hobbies, sports teams, places or practices. Adherents of these topics read the groups and can respond to other posts and join in the discussion. Jealously guarded by their first users, newsgroups have now proliferated widely and most Internet users have access to tens of thousands of different groups. Since the system is essentially unregulated and mostly unmoderated, there is considerable illegal activity, particularly in the form of pornography, to be found in these areas.

This should not suggest however that Usenet is not regulated at all, even if this regulation is rather more complex than an externally imposed regime. In her study of the alt.folklore.urban (AFU) newsgroup, Michele Tepper makes pertinent comments about newsgroup behaviour. She is perceptive in her analysis of 'trolling', whereby a message is posted which will lead those not in the know to react inappropriately. Trolling, she says, 'serves the dual purpose of enforcing community standards and of increasing community cohesion by providing a game that all those who know the rules can play against those who do not' (Tepper, 1997: 40). She also reminds her readers of what an appropriate term 'trolling' is, since it originally meant the practice of leaving a boat with a baited fishing line overboard to see what might bite, and she makes a persuasive case for the possibility of community within non-synchronous environments.

> Usenet is not a particularly propitious space in which to form any long-term community in the first place, and this may be part of the reason why research on virtual communities has instead focussed on sites for realtime interaction such as MUDs/MOOs and IRC channels. However, any user of LISTSERV mailing lists, bulletin boards, and Usenet newsgroups can tell you that virtual communities arise in these non-realtime arenas as well. Although a discussion composed of discrete postings lacks the immediacy that many find so alluring about realtime sites, it has an advantage over these latter in that the membership of the community is not constrained by the logistics of who can log on when. Time lags in the conversation allow for the formation of

e-mail back channels between group regulars that help promote conversational intimacy among the regulars.

(Tepper, 1997: 44)

Much of the role previously played by newsgroups is now taken by the Web Forum or Bulletin Board, itself a development of the BBS (Bulletin Board Systems) of the 1970s and 1980s. Web Forums are structured message sites which have developed from the earlier newsgroups and Bulletin Boards, and which assume that a discourse will follow the pattern of an initial statement, which then receives replies, which can themselves then be replied to. This essentially asynchronous branching structure is found on many Web sites. Such message boards and forums are particularly popular where the owner is hoping to make contact with users in different time zones, perhaps involving communication between Europe and the USA.

Into the Dungeons

Multi-modal texts within the information technology world have traditionally been characterised as adventure stories or modelling activities where readers have choices to make and decisions to consider which will affect future outcomes. In its most characteristic version, this results in the branching story of the kind popular in the early 1970s in book form. A reader is presented with a situation or problem, and given a choice of alternative responses. The choice of response leads to a further set of responses, and so on. This type of environment can be unwieldy in book form, since it involves much frantic page-switching back and forth and always allows for the apparent cheating involved in checking the outcome of alternative responses. The computerised version is much more constraining and seems more like an infinite variety of adventures devised by the reader, although this is a deception since there will always be a finite although possibly very large number of different adventures or stories which are possible.

A further development of the branching computer-based narrative has been the MUD (Multi-User Domains or Dungeons) phenomenon in which participants exist and interact in an imaginary and overtly literary world, derived from fantasy and science-fiction genres, and subject to complex rules and conventions. MUDs and their offshoots have identity construction and maintenance as their main rationale, although there is a clear recognition that these identities are assumed. There is far less ambiguity about identity and reality on MUDs than there is in some of the later environments that are Web-based.

The typical MUD has been described as 'an heroic attempt to recreate in prose what its users would prefer to be a sensory experience' (Bolter,

1996: 109). Textually based only because the technology can barely cope yet with the video experience that must certainly follow, these environments are destined to become 'multiuser, networked virtual realities' (Bolter, 1996: 109).

MUDs have had a troubled history. Reminding us that they have been banned in Australia, Beaubien indicates that this 'freewheeling fantasy play' (Beaubien, 1996: 181) may have its seamy side. Beaubien is among many writers (Beaubien, 1996; Dibbell, 1994; Mackinnon, 1997; Spender, 1995; Turkle, 1996) who have referred to the now notorious case of what has come to be known as the LambdaMOO virtual rape. Although there are certainly important points to be made about this deeply unpleasant story, it is striking that this one incident should appear in so many commentaries, leading one to surmise that perhaps such incidents are not so common as some commentators would aim to suggest. The fact that this incident happened in a community inhabited, at the time, by those who were in most cases university lecturers is in no small part responsible for the number of academic papers and references which relate to this topic. Quantitative data on the prevalence of such behaviour, which might describe the extent and importance of the phenomenon, is remarkably difficult to find.

Beaubien also continues his account beyond the immediate reaction, unlike many other writers, and describes what happened after the incident. Rather than the 'virtual rape' having led to the necessity for outside controls from the real world, the members of the MOO in fact chose to develop virtual controls that would operate within the conventions of the environment they had built. Inappropriate behaviour was dealt with not by the inner self controls described as 'face' (Brown and Levinson, 1987) but by the adoption of virtual controls, part of the MOO process of 'constructing reality' (Beaubien, 1996). New rules were generated as to the process by which characters could be created and removed, with designated individuals given the electronic rights to remove a character that was causing offence to a large number of individuals. In this way, participants built an imaginary system of laws on to an imaginary world of actors and events.

Among the most famous and developed of online environments, the LambdaMOO has been much discussed ever since the virtual rape incident in the 1980s. Virtual and stateless but always essentially Californian, the LambdaMOO began at Xerox in Paolo Alto and its community structure bears a joint heritage based on Californian lifestyles and the Dungeons and Dragons book and gaming community which is its most obvious precursor. In the definitive study of the LambdaMOO, Julian Dibbell describes it from the perspective of a participant-observer and notes that even the Dungeons and Dragons manual advised the adoption of a near trance-like state when experiencing the online environment. Dungeons and Dragons players, he suggests, were 'not merely represented by their richly detailed characters – they were identified with them' (Dibbell, 1998: 55).

Writing as a participant in the LambdaMOO, Dibbell talks about himself in the third person and describes his feelings when online.

> These intense, late-night VR [virtual reality] conversations, he has noticed, have a funny way of messing with the language circuits in his brain. Something about the ambiguity of the medium, he figures, about the way it hovers between speech and writing. After a couple of hours glued to monitor and keyboard trading words as fast as finger muscles will allow, he can sometimes start to feel a kind of meltdown going on inside him, as if the part of him that usually does the talking and the part of him that usually does the writing are getting all mixed up together. Sometimes the feeling lingers after he has logged off, and he wakes up the next day with a throatful of writerly cadences and two-dollar words waiting to be coughed up like morning phlegm.
>
> (Dibbell, 1998: 121)

Gender swapping, very much a part of life in most online communities, was equally present in LambdaMOO practice.

> the payoffs of cross-gendered MOOing for male players were many and varied, and potentially rather knotty. Some players, of course, simply enjoyed the extra attention given to women in any social setting, and especially in one where men outnumbered them by about two to one. Others liked the challenge of deception, testing the limits of their ability to pass for female. ... Still others came to value the experience as a glimpse of life on the far side of the gender gap – a firsthand, eye-opening sampler of the routine harassments, double-edged perks, and broad-brushed preconceptions most women encounter every day. And naturally there were many players in whom any number of these sometimes contradictory motivations could be found commingling to one degree or another, which may begin to give you some idea of what a tricky proposition it could be to say just what was going on when real-life boys got it into their heads to become virtual girls.
>
> (Dibbell, 1998: 131)

Young People, Virtual Communities and the Business World

Voices from the business world have increasingly predicted change in other areas, particularly education. In his second book, Bill Gates addressed education less centrally than he had in *The Road Ahead*, but he still describes a situation in some US campuses in which the Web is already the lattice that links all areas of education.

Gates is refreshingly honest about how long it took for Microsoft to recognise the importance of the Internet. He describes how, in 1993, the whole Microsoft Web site was hosted on three computers on a folding table in a hallway, 'with hand-written instructions on how to connect to the Internet' (Gates, 1999: 164). It was the business world, and Coca-Cola in particular, that first embraced e-mail. Gates describes how the Coca-Cola company had its own internal e-mail system from the 1980s and goes on to admire the way in which the company decided in 1997 to standardise all its use of IT systems worldwide – standardising, one presumes, on Microsoft Windows.

Young people, of course, flocked to the Internet in large numbers before Microsoft and others finally recognised that this was a phenomenon that would not be transitory in its effects. More recently, attempts have been made to consider whether online life is truly community based. An essential question would appear to be the extent to which young Web publishers represent an identifiable community which, although not geographically located, has all the other characteristics of what some writers (Jones, 1995) have come to describe as cybersocieties.

Jones quotes previously defined characteristics of a community (Etzioni, 1991) as being scope, substance and dominance. If we apply these aspects to online communities we find a high degree of congruence, or even compliance, if we view these communities as rule-bound and joined through agreement to keep those rules. The Web publishing community, in particular, has a defined scope: that of those people who have access to the reading and writing tools and the necessary technology to make use of them. Content is highly differentiated and specific to this community, in that it deals with topics and references of interest to readers. Subtle and pervasive strategies of dominance underpin the community in the form of software upgrades, leading to high dominance for those who use the latest plug-ins or add-ons. Even a government educational body such as the UK School Curriculum and Assessment Authority (SCAA) informed readers of its Web page in 1996 that they should have the latest version of the Netscape Navigator browser in order to see the site at its best.

Where young Web page designers are concerned, these pressures were seen in the references to particular browsers needed to see a page properly, and the team loyalty which soon built up as the range of browsers became a straightforward choice between Netscape Navigator and Microsoft Internet Explorer. Ownership of a page requiring the latest RealAudio or streamed video plug-in not only transmits a certain image to readers, it also leads them to feel that they should be using these technologies.

Jones (1995) describes computer-mediated communication (CMC) as 'one means ... with which we can fly in and out of societies' and he could be talking about the creation of homepages when he goes on to say:

> Because these machines are seen as 'linking' machines ... they inherently affect the ways we think of linking up to each other, and thus they fit squarely into our concerns about society. Media technologies that have largely been tied to the 'transportation' view of communication mentioned earlier were developed to overcome space and time. The computer, in particular, is an 'efficiency' machine, purporting to ever increase its speed. But unlike those technologies, the computer used for communication is a technology to be understood from the 'ritual' view of communication, for once time and space have been overcome (or at least rendered surmountable) the spur for development is connection, linkage. Once we can surmount time and space and 'be' anywhere, we must choose a 'where' at which to be, and the computer's functionality lies in its power to make us organise our desires about the spaces we visit and stay in.
>
> (Jones, 1995: 32)

Nevertheless, it is not the ability to move through time and space that defines the computer's communicable abilities so much as the huge range of texts that embody the process of communication itself. From this perspective the texts themselves, traces of conversation and writing, are crucial to any analysis of online community.

The online communities and those individuals who chose to publish on the Web in the early years were not representative of the whole chronological, geographical and social world community. They were in the majority of cases young, male, middle class and either American or European. Many of the first users to see the potential of Web publishing do seem to have been lonely young people. On their Web pages authors frequently wrote about the potential they felt was offered by the Web.

> I once was isolated and lonely, and the 'net really helped give me solace and find some value in a world that sometimes seems tempestuous. The advent of home pages gives me an outlet to distribute my thoughts, ideas, and feelings – something so many people on here gave me so much of. Don't begin to think that I believe the net is a supplement for real human interaction. I think it's a complement that can sometimes be a little detrimental. Computers are great when you're just beginning to see light and building the confidence to come out of your shell. But one shouldn't stagnate in the Web – it's not some opiate form of human interaction. Computer interaction is so paradoxical –

you feel so close yet so far. When one begins to embrace fonts a little too much, it's time to return to reality.

> (Male, 17 years, USA, personal homepage, January 1996)

There is much to discuss here, but for the present purpose it is enough to recognise the apparent motive for publication: an expressed desire to form part of a more caring community. A description of the contents of a few more Web homepages will illustrate the wide range of uses to which this publishing medium is being put. First of all, many appear to be building on the features of Internet language previously described in synchronous communication (Abbott, 1996) and have written their texts in an assumed dialect which can be almost impenetrable to outsiders. A young British Web user who uses this specialised form of language is also aware of its impenetrability for some readers. Helpfully, he therefore provides a summary in standard English.

> If any of you have any ideas for a theme to my page, then send 'em in Matee'o's and if ya' 'ave any pics ta go wiv 'em, den by all means giv 'em 'ere! DUDE!

> What I meant was, if you can think of a good theme for me to base my page on, then I would be grateful for them.
> (Male, 14 years, UK, personal homepage, January 1996)

The introduction to an American user's homepage is written in a vernacular that was fast becoming, at least in the mid-1990s, the primary mode of textual composition on the World Wide Web.

> So you're out surfing, raisin' a little hell with your computer, and where do you find yourself but on my homepage. Not your homepage, see, this place is home to no one but myself. Beware, ye weak of soul, ye weak of heart, ye weak of ling! Like Lord Byron, I'm mad, bad and DANGEROUS to know.
> (Male, 18 yrs, USA, personal homepage, January 1996)

Some critics have seen confirmation through this community's apparent abandonment of rules of the essentially insupportable nature of grammar and spelling. Although not all would go as far as Spender (1995) in this approach, many might agree that the functional aspects of traditional grammar are increasingly under threat and difficult to defend. Noting that the standardisation of spelling and grammar can be seen as a direct outcome of the arrival of the printing press, Spender also conjectures that what she sees as the current decline of the print medium will mean that such standardised rules and conventions will begin to relax their hold.

The dismay and distress at the passing of the print era has more to do with bringing to an end a patriarchal presence that has been encoded in communication than it has to do with the loss of print.

(Spender, 1995: 10)

The Arrival of Webrings: Organising the Environment

By the late 1990s, online communities were no longer self-creating but sometimes formed with the help of structures created by Internet businesses, particularly those concerned with creating the portal sites which were seen then as the key to success in electronic commerce. Notions such as that of the Webring (http:// www.webring.org), where hobbyists sharing pages about a common topic choose to band together and publicise their membership of a particular interest group, became extremely popular as Internet users sought to find a marked way through the vast wastes of online existence.

More recently, the development of advertising-funded commercial communities such as Angelfire and Geocities has created a new although rather artificial situation. These sites offer a home for Web pages and are financed not by subscriptions but by the fees paid by the advertisers whose banners appears on the pages stored on the company's server. A similar opportunity has arisen through the addition not only of Web page creation facilities but also of community structures to online services such as America Online and CompuServe. A further dimension has been added with the development of ersatz Webring systems such as the Net Circles on America Online; Webrings were devised by a commercially funded organisation but hand over considerable control to the user.

Webrings and Net Circles are online metaphors for self-selected groups of people who consider that their homepages have something in common. Typically, one homepage owner with an interest in, say, historic steam engines will invite two other such homepage owners to join his Webring. Anyone who enters 'steam engine' into the Webring search engine will be directed to a listing of these three sites. If that person also has a homepage about steam engines, he (for in this case it would almost certainly be he) can then join the Webring, a process which is accomplished automatically after he fills in an online form. In this way, many Webrings quickly gain a membership of several hundred, although the more populated ones tend to then break up into subdivisions of the topic involved.

What has developed is a situation where two major developments are in conflict: commercially provided facilities and a rapidly learning non-commercial collective of (often) young people. This complex situation has had a number of effects. In the first case there are now many more Web sites which apparently belong to or are part of online communities. They make this clear through buttons or logos and by linking to others in the community, and through index pages for the group. However, it is difficult to tell whether this community belonging is analogous to the previous searching for community in the early days of the Web, or is something much more mundane and merely indicates a desire to use facilities that are offered. Within many homepage systems, for example, it is possible to use one of a set of standard Web wallpaper backgrounds, or the user can create a new one: but in most cases, one of the default offerings is selected. One of the effects of this development of templates is that many Web pages now look like many other Web pages.

Communities have members but they also, by their very nature, resist some aspirants who may attempt to enter. The notion of the lurker, the outsider who listens in – or reads in – but does not participate, has largely been superseded by the membership conventions that are springing up on most of the apparently free but advertising-funded Web sites. The faintly derogatory sound of the term 'lurker' has been seen (Lee, 1996) as a facet of the hostility shown to outsiders, and the use of the term 'newbie' for a recent online arrival represents a similar resistance to others joining.

Chapter Summary

- Communities no longer need to be based in a geographical site and it is not necessary for people to meet physically in order to feel part of a community.
- The telephone and short-wave radio created virtual communities too; but not to the extent now found through the use of computers and the Internet.
- For young people, community adherence is often linked to issues of identity.
- Young adolescents may use computers to help create their own identity.
- Online community can exist in asynchronous as well as realtime communication sites.
- Online communities tend to reject imposed regulations and to develop their own self-imposed rules.
- Many young people find online communities more welcoming than some of their real-life counterparts.

Bibliography

Abbott, C. (1996). *Young People Developing a New Language: The Implications for Teachers and for Education of Electronic Discourse*. Paper presented at Euro Education '96, Aalborg, Denmark.

—— (1999). *The Internet, Text Production and the Construction of Identity: Changing Use by Young Males during the early to mid 1990s*. Unpublished PhD, King's College, University of London.

Beaubien, M. (1996). Playing at community: multi-user dungeons and social interaction in cyberspace. In L. Strate (ed.), *Communications and Cyberspace* (179–88). Cresskill, NJ: Hampton Press.

Bolter, J. D. (1996). Virtual reality and the redefinition of self. In L. Strate (ed.), *Communications in Cyberspace* (105–20). Cresskill, NJ: Hampton Press.

Brown, P. and Levinson, S. (1987). *Politeness: Some Universals in Language Usage*. Cambridge: Cambridge University Press.

Cutler, R. H. (1996). Technologies, relations and selves. In L. Strate (ed.), *Communications and Cyberspace* (317–32). Cresskill, NJ: Hampton Press.

Dibbell, J. (1994). A rape in cyberspace; or, how an evil clown, a Haitian trickster spirit, two wizards, and a cast of dozens turned a database into a society. In M. Dery (ed.), *Flame Wars: The Discourse of Cyberculture* (237–62). Durham, NC: Duke University Press.

—— (1998). *My Tiny Life: Crime and Passion in a Virtual World*. London: Fourth Estate.

Downes, T. (1996). The computer as a toy and tool in the home: implications for schools and teachers. *Education and Information Technologies*, 1, 191–201.

Etzioni, A. (1991). *The Responsive Society*. San Francisco: Jossey-Bass.

Foster, D. (1997). Community and Identity in the Electronic Village. In D. Porter (ed.), *Internet Culture* (23–38). New York: Routledge.

Gates, B. (1999). *Business Using a Digital Nervous System*. London: Penguin Books.

Gergen, K. J. (1991). *The Saturated Self: Dilemmas of Identity in Contemporary Life*. New York: HarperCollins.

Head, J. (1997). *Working with Adolescents: Constructing Identity*. London: Falmer Press.

Healy, D. (1997). Cyberspace and Place: The Internet as Middle Landscape on the Electronic Frontier. In D. Porter (ed.), *Internet Culture* (55–68). New York: Routledge.

Jones, S. G. (ed.) (1995). *Cybersociety: Computer-mediated Communication and Community*. London: Sage.

—— (ed.) (1997). *Virtual Culture: Identity and Communication in Cybersociety*. London: Sage.

Lanham, R. (1994). *The Electronic Word: Democracy, Technology, and the Arts*. Chicago: University of Chicago Press.

Lee, J. Y. (1996). Charting the codes of cyberspace: a rhetoric of electronic mail. In L. Strate (ed.), *Communications and Cyberspace* (275–96). Cresskill, NJ: Hampton Press.

Lipton, M. (1996). Forgetting the body: cybersex and identity. In L. Strate (ed.), *Communications and Cyberspace* (335–50). Cresskill, NJ: Hampton Press.

Ludlow, P. (ed.) (1996). *High Noon on the Electronic Frontier: Conceptual Issues in Cyberspace*. Cambridge, MA: The MIT Press.

Mackinnon, R. C. (1997). Punishing the persona: correctional strategies for the virtual offender. In S. G. Jones (ed.), *Virtual Culture: Identity and Communication in Cybersociety* (206–35). London: Sage.

Meyerowitz, J. (1985). *No Sense of Place: The Impact of Electronic Media on Social Behaviour*. New York: Oxford University Press.

Porter, D. (ed.) (1997). *Internet Culture*. London: Routledge.

Rheingold, H. (1993). *Virtual Communities: Homesteading on the Electronic Frontier*. New York: Harper Perennial.

—— (1996). A Slice of My Life in My Virtual Community. In P. Ludlow (ed.), *High Noon on the Electronic Frontier*. Cambridge, MA: The MIT Press.

Sefton-Green, J. (ed.) (1998). *Digital Diversions: Youth Culture in the Age of Multimedia*. London: UCL Press.

Shields, R. (ed.) (1996). *Cultures of Internet: Virtual Spaces, Real Histories, Living Bodies*. London: Sage.

Spender, D. (1995). *Nattering on the Net: Women, Power and Cyberspace*. Melbourne: Spinifex Press.

Tapscott, D. (1998). *Growing up Digital: The rise of the Net Generation*. New York: McGraw-Hill.

Tepper, M. (1997). Usenet communities and the cultural politics of information. In D. Porter (ed.), *Internet Culture* (39–54). New York: Routledge.

Turkle, S. (1984). *Second Self: Computers and the Human Spirit*. New York: Simon & Schuster.

—— (1996). *Life on the Screen: Identity in the Age of the Internet*. London: Weidenfield & Nicholson.

Wilbur, S. P. (1997). An archaeology of cyberpaces: virtuality, community, identity. In D. Porter (ed.), *Internet Culture* (5–22). New York: Routledge.

3 Changing Schools

It is not without significance that we use the same word – school – to describe the process our children undergo and the physical location in which it takes place; or we have, at any rate, done so until very recently. We have assumed that it is only by attending this special place, different from the real world, and staffed by experts, that our young people can be taught. It is teaching, and the schools in which it takes place, that forms the focus for this chapter; the extent to which learning has also changed through technology will be discussed more fully in chapter 4.

Teachers, then, come to the fore in our discussion of schools, for it is they who are the givers of understanding or founts of knowledge from which our children are popularly supposed to drink; but this is not an unchallenged assumption.

> A ... major illusion on which the school system rests is that most learning is the result of teaching. Teaching, it is true, may contribute to certain kinds of learning under certain circumstances. But most people acquire most of their knowledge outside school, and in school only in so far as school, in a few rich countries, has become their place of confinement during an increasing part of their lives.
>
> (Illich, 1973: 20)

Writing in the 1970s, Illich was describing a system in another country and indeed in another age, but much that he had to say thirty years ago enables us to look anew at current developments of our notions of what school might be. It is for this reason that a number of Illich's proposals will be revisited in this chapter in order to consider whether they still sound quite as outlandish and unrealistic as they seemed to many when they were first published. His views may be extreme, especially here when he generalises about knowledge acquisition, but it is sometimes by refuting the extent of a statement that we understand the underlying truth of it.

This chapter begins with a discussion of the concept of the school and some history of the introduction of computers into the classroom in the UK. This history is more correctly that of the development of computers in England, for it is one of the many inconsistencies and surprises of this history that, in many cases, the development has been subtly but importantly different in Scotland and sometimes in Northern Ireland and Wales. This is particularly true when discussing the impact of the National Curriculum and of government funding schemes, which have often been managed and controlled to different agendas within Departments of Education and the Scottish Office; a precursor, perhaps, of more extensive differences as the UK moves into an era of devolved regional government.

School Size and Learning

In medieval times, as Illich reminds us, education was 'complex, lifelong and unplanned' (Illich, 1973: 29), but it is only quite recently that politicians and educational thinkers have begun seriously to reconsider the notion of lifelong learning. For the last hundred years or more the school building, in the UK and most of the developed world, has been seen as the only or most vital site for learning. Countries around the world have developed systems of schooling which have often been based on the systems in place in colonial powers and usually related to a linear series of schools. In most cases these begin with small institutions and progress to much larger ones as the child gets older. Many adults will remember their own reaction to this period of schooling as being not dissimilar to that of Illich when he reminds us of the apparent reward for such compliance: 'school is obligatory and becomes schooling for schooling's sake: an enforced stay in the company of teachers, which pays off in the doubtful privilege of more such company' (Illich, 1973: 24).

For many children in the twentieth century, formal education began somewhere around the age of 5 to 7 in a building with perhaps less than a hundred pupils. By the age of 11, that child might be being educated alongside a few hundred others; and by the age of 16 alongside as many as one or two thousand. Entry into further or higher education could mean a further jump to a learning community of many thousands of students. By the end of the twentieth century there were serious concerns about the effectiveness of this model for all children. The home-school movement, discussed in chapter 4, grew throughout the second half of the century, but gained renewed resources and the confidence of community support through the use of networked technology. For the majority of children, however, the twenty-first century began as had the twentieth, with daily attendance within a school building for a period of ten years or more.

Classroom attendance removes children from the everyday world of Western culture and plunges them into an environment far more primitive, magical and deadly serious. School could not create such an enclave within which the rules of ordinary reality are suspended, unless it physically incarcerated the young during many successive years on sacred territory.

(Illich, 1973: 39)

The driving factor for much of the gradual increase in establishment size has been characterised as the need to provide particular resources, especially in the form of libraries and specialist teaching. In the UK, school libraries probably saw their highest point in the 1970s, with large numbers of school librarians housed in new buildings which put libraries at their core. Selective schools had always done this, of course, but the alternative schools in selective systems, the secondary moderns, had very little in the way of library resources by comparison. The rise of the comprehensive school in the 1970s was in many cases the mechanism by which better library facilities were made available to children, but by the 1980s and 1990s spending on books was falling in real terms year by year.

Libraries, in schools and in local communities, have adopted technology in a piecemeal way, but the initiatives of the Blair government have begun to see a role for the library in education, with significant funding available to provide some equipment for libraries, to train librarians and to pay for the development of online content.

Even without the rapid development of computer-mediated information there would have been likely to be continuing concerns about the validity of Victorian models of schooling. Once computers began offering a new medium with which to support and mediate schooling, real changes were able to occur in the delivery and support of formal education. Change, however, has always seemed threatening to our educational systems and to those who control them. As was suggested by Postman (Postman and Weingartner, 1971), it is the failure to recognise that change is the normal state for the world which has bedevilled the educational system, although it should be noted that he talks for the most part about the US system, and as it was in the 1970s.

Schools and Technology

Chapter 5 discusses in some detail the response of schools to the availability of technology of all kinds, and it is clear that the relationship has been, for the most part, deeply ambivalent. Perhaps the most crucial reason for this has been the range of different models of computer use that have been internalised by teachers and learners. As will be shown later, the teaching machines of the 1960s have had a long-lasting effect on the teachers who attended schools then, giving them a touching faith in the ability of the machine to teach, a faith not yet supportable in practice.

As a result, for many teachers, technology has been about machines taking the place of teachers. It is hardly surprising, then, that they have sometimes been ambivalent about these devices and have not always seemed to welcome them into their classrooms. Now that the prevailing mood is changing, with even the relatively conservative model of most of the New Opportunities Fund training programmes being that of computer as tool rather than teacher, it is likely that real change could follow in teacher perceptions and expectations.

Illich suggested that 'Technology is available to develop either independence and learning or bureaucracy and teaching' (Illich, 1973: 80) and technology in the latter area has been well developed in the UK, which is hardly surprising in a country which has spent much of the last two hundred years developing bureaucracy into something approaching an art form. Schools were given high-specification computers for logging attendance, creating statistical returns and submitting examination entries by e-mail long before similar tools became available in the classroom.

The emphasis throughout the 1980s on administrative uses of the computer in education did have one useful though unexpected outcome. Headteachers, whose role in the UK has become increasingly that of administrators rather than curriculum managers, learnt a great deal from their own use of computer technology as a productivity tool. When advisers, of which I was one, arrived in schools to talk about classroom use of productivity tools such as word processors and databases, they found to their surprise that it was often the headteacher who had the most developed understanding of the possibilities of such resources. It was only with the gradual increase in teacher ownership of PCs that such understanding moved across the teaching force as a whole. It was disappointing to many observers that far-sighted moves such as the provision of laptop computers to every teacher in the Australian state of Victoria were followed in 2000 in the UK only by half-hearted attempts to provide 50 per cent of the purchase price (less VAT and income tax) of a laptop for 10 per cent of the teaching force.

Computers and Education in England – 1999–2002

The Government is fully committed to ensuring that all schools and teachers are in a position to deploy new information and communication technologies (ICT) to raise educational standards to enhance learning and to prepare young people with the ICT skills they will need in society and at work in the twenty-first century.

(DfEE, 1998: 3)

With these words, the UK government, in a recent summary of statistics in this area, indicates how far it has come in its understanding of the power of ICT. Alongside many other European countries, the UK entered the twenty-first century in the throes of a major programme of equipping schools and training teachers. As in Sweden, the UK planned to provide in-service training in the use of ICT for all its teachers. The actual training provided was quite different, however. In the UK, each teacher could cash in a voucher worth £500 for a training course lasting the equivalent of two or three days and which was usually delivered for the most part through distance education, meaning that the teachers took part in their own time. On completion of the course, teachers might qualify for the 50 per cent grant towards computer purchase, provided they do so as part of the first 10 per cent of teachers to be trained. In Sweden, the equivalent course lasted several weeks, and successful completion led to the receipt of a laptop computer, but funds were available to train only half of the country's teaching force. A further big difference was that the scheme in Sweden was voluntary, whereas all teachers in the UK are expected to take part in the training, or show that they do not need it, by 2002.

By 1999, then, the Government was able to boast of an ICT in education programme which was 'the most ambitious ever undertaken in terms of targets and investments' (DfEE, 1999: 3). The investment described amounted to over £1.6 billion between 1999 and 2002, and was used to provide the described training for all serving teachers, and to upgrade significantly the equipment found in schools, colleges and libraries. The involvement of libraries is important in terms of this being a marker of growing awareness at governmental level that schools cannot remain alone as sites of formal education in the future. This recognition has, in part, led to the developments described in chapter 7.

The DfEE ICT Survey takes place each year and bases its conclusions on a random sample of schools. It reports only on schools in England; statistics for the other UK countries are either not collected or are collected separately. The most recent survey showed that by early 1999 there were an average of sixteen computers in each primary school, 101 in each secondary school and twenty-one in each special school. These average figures seem fairly unhelpful when set against the widely varying sizes of different schools, and the figure more usually quoted is the average computer–pupil ratio, giving schools a bench-mark against which they can compare their own provision (see Table 1).

Table 1   Computer–pupil ratio (pupils per computer) 1998–9

	1998	*1999*
Primary	18	13
Secondary	9	8
Special	4	4

Source: DfEE (1999: 6)

This group of ratios, amongst the most favourable anywhere in the world and matched only in Canada, the USA and a few European countries, has been achieved as a result of considerable and continuing investment. The survey noted that, leaving aside expenditure on ICT for administrative purposes, the average secondary school was spending £38,200 per year on ICT for teaching and learning in 1999. The primary and special figures were £5,700 and £9,674 per year. These figures do not, of course, include staff costs. Once again, it is only the average spend per pupil which gives schools a total with which to compare their own spending (see Table 2). As can be seen from the table, the most startling rise has been in expenditure at the primary level. It is also this sector that has shown the most marked change in the proportion of schools connected to the Internet (see Table 3).

Table 2   Average expenditure on ICT per pupil (not including school management and administration) 1998–9

	1998	*1999*
Primary	£11	£27
Secondary	£38	£45
Special	£73	£124

Source: DfEE (1999: 12)

Table 3   Percentage of schools connected to the Internet 1998–9

	1998 (per cent)	*1999 (per cent)*
Primary	17	62
Secondary	83	93
Special	31	60

Source: DfEE (1999: 18)

The area of the survey which describes teacher use of ICT is that which is most relevant to any examination of changes in education driven by ICT. Early 1999 was too early for the trend towards computer rooms in primary schools to have shown up in the findings, and this is borne out by the figures given for deployment of computers. In secondary schools, 43 per cent of computers were in an ICT room, whereas the figure for primary schools was only 12 per cent (and 17 per cent for special schools).

The DfEE Survey's Table 15 (reproduced here: see Table 4) indicates use of ICT by subject in each category of school. Apart from the confident finding that ICT is used at least a little for the teaching of English and

Mathematics in every primary school in the country, this table also suggests that the major use of ICT in primary schools is for the core subjects. For secondary schools it is for the other foundation subjects

Table 4:   Use of IT in the curriculum (percentage of schools)

Primary	Substantial	Some	Little	None
English	52	44	3	–
Maths	22	66	12	–
Science	6	55	35	3
D & T	1	27	48	23
History	7	50	35	8
Geography	3	50	43	4
Art	10	47	35	8
Music	1	21	46	32
PE	0	1	10	89
RE	–	11	38	51
Other	2	2	3	20
Secondary	Substantial	Some	Little	None
English	9	59	31	1
Maths	7	55	36	2
Science	6	57	36	2
D & T	34	51	15	1
History	3	45	45	6
Geography	6	53	38	3
Art/Design	6	34	50	10
Music	17	39	33	11
PE	3	18	50	29
RE	3	30	53	13
MFL	7	38	50	6
Business Studies	69	23	6	2
IT	98	2	0	0

Source: DfEE (1999: Table 15)
Notes: – denotes negligible, i.e. less than 0.5%

outside the core. The data relating to special schools has not been included since it is rarely appropriate to generalise on subject issues in that context.

Leaving aside some of the puzzling figures here, such as the 2 per cent of schools who do not use ICT substantially when teaching Information Technology or the 2 per cent (possibly the same 2 per cent) who never use computers when teaching Business Studies, there are other differences to be seen between the ways that the different stages of schooling use ICT.

It is clear that the use of ICT within English is extremely well established in primary schools, with no other substantial subject use even approaching the same level of penetration. The difference on reaching secondary school is startling, with only 9 per cent of secondary schools making substantial use of ICT in English. It is Music, perhaps surprisingly, which has the next highest proportion of schools making substantial use of ICT in the subject, perhaps an indication of the changes in the means by which sound is created, manipulated and reproduced. Digital sound technology and word processing appear to be the technical developments which have had most effect on the curriculum. As might be expected, the majority of schools use at least some ICT in the core subjects of English, Mathematics and Science, as well as in the technology-related disciplines of Design and Technology and Business Studies.

Activity

Look at the table of school use of ICT within subjects.

- Why are the differences between subjects so different between primary and secondary sectors?
- Mathematics was the subject which first used ICT, so why might the figures for use of ICT be comparatively low?
- How might these figures change as a result of the training for all teachers and the extra equipment that has now been installed in schools?
- Obtain a copy of the 2000 DfEE ICT Survey and see how these figures have changed.

Around two-thirds of all teachers were reported in the survey to be confident users of ICT. This is a heartening picture, although one not always borne out by other surveys in other contexts, as will be shown. Even more surprisingly, the figures seemed to be remarkably similar across primary, secondary and special schools, although the rate and style of ICT use is very different in each sector. One reason for this could be inequitable access or resourcing, so the findings in Table 5 do indicate a hopeful future as far as resources are concerned.

Table 5   Teacher confidence (percentage who feel confident to use ICT within the curriculum)

	1998	1999
Primary	65	68
Secondary	61	66
Special	65	68

Source: DfEE (1999): 18

There has been criticism, however, of the nature of this teacher ICT confidence. In particular, much of the survey is filled in by headteachers, heads of department and subject coordinators. A teacher rated as confident by her head of department may not rate herself quite so highly, for confidence is a subjective concept. The British Educational Suppliers Association (BESA) also conducts an annual survey of ICT use in schools, and their most recent survey produced very different results on the topic of teacher confidence, as discussed by Dominic Savage, BESA Chief Executive, in his address to the Resource Conference, Doncaster in November 1999 (see Table 6).

Table 6   Percentage of all teachers currently confident/
           competent in the use of ICT

Primary	47
Secondary	35
Special	42

Source: Savage (1999)

Savage noted with concern, as did the BESA Survey, the low confidence figure for secondary. We could also ask exactly what it was that the teachers did or did not feel confident in doing; and it may be that secondary teachers set higher goals for themselves in this area. In his address, Savage referred to persistent but anecdotal evidence that some departments in secondary schools use almost no ICT at all. Even more disturbingly, he claimed that some departments were actually using less ICT at Key Stage 4, mainly due to the failure of the examination boards to recognise the existence of ICT in any meaningful sense.

The BESA Survey, a postal survey of 1883 schools, asks many questions which are not asked by the DfEE exercise, as would be expected in an activity designed mainly to inform its corporate membership. Software developers, for example, are interested in total numbers of computers as well as the way in which they are distributed in schools, and BESA provides the figures for this, both for 1999 and for 2000, relying on schools' ability to predict for the rest of the financial year (see Table 7).

Table 7   Computers in UK schools 1999-2000

	June 1999	*April 2000*
Primary	363,300	404,000
Secondary	510,000	565,000
Special	31,000	33,200
Total	904,000	1,002,000

Source: Savage (1999)

As well as providing the headline-grabbing figure of a million computers in UK schools at the turn of the century, these figures also provide a base from which Savage calculates the optimum number of computers within each category of schools, which he calculates to be 506,000 (primary), 700,000 (secondary) and 36,500 (special), a total of 1,242,000 computers in UK schools.

The Background to this Picture

Computers, then, have become seen as generic tools for learning which have relevance across the curriculum. They have not always been seen in this emancipatory way. For many years, they were the technology associated with a particular discipline, often known as Computer Science or Computer Studies, with the disagreements as to which was the better term providing a precursor to the later arguments between the proponents of Information Technology (IT) and Information and Communication Technologies (ICT).

It was in the 1970s that education authorities in schools began to install computer terminals, primitive machines that predated the desktop PC and which were capable of only the most routine of tasks. The Inner London Education Authority (ILEA) was among the first to develop this area, and also appointed the first inspector for computer education in 1972. At that time twelve secondary schools in London were connected through telephone lines to a large computer in an office block in the Tottenham Court Road used only for mathematics education. By 1990, when the ILEA was abolished and the London boroughs took over responsibility for education, much had been achieved.

> ILEA will bequeath to the Inner London Boroughs in April 1990 a situation in which every single school, together with numerous support units and other agencies, will have a range of computer equipment which stands comparison with the best in commerce and industry, while satisfying the needs peculiar to education. From the support provided by one individual seventeen years ago there is now a team of eighty, working from the Inner London Educational Computing Centre (ILECC). Thousands of teachers have received training. Much educational support material has been produced. The National Curriculum places information technology as a central element of every subject, as well as a discipline in its own right with a distinct profile component. If its requirements are to be met, support at this level will need to be maintained.
>
> (Esterson, 1989)

This statement from ILEA Education Officer David Mallen in his fore-word to a booklet summarising progress in school computer use by 1989 was an indicator of the battles ahead. ILECC did continue, but only for a few years; I was by then its Director having been leading the Curriculum Support team for several years. Despite the leadership of one London LEA and the support of many others, the changed climate of education in the early 1990s and the diminishing role of the LEA support sector led to ILECC's closure in 1994. Today there are very few support services provided by LEAs in London and in some other parts of the UK, although some of the large and medium-sized LEAs have managed to maintain their centres. One example of the extent of the change is that over forty advisory teachers solely for IT and Special Needs were appointed to UK LEAs in 1988; within five years none of them remained in post.

The early years of computer use in schools were accompanied by considerable use of drill and practice programs, themselves the descendants of the activities delivered through microfiche and microfilm in teaching machines, a topic to which we will return in chapter 5. Much of the development of the use of computers to support learning has been bedevilled by those who have misunderstood their uses and have then claimed that they can in some way act as teachers. The work of researchers such as Seymour Papert has sometimes been cited to support these claims, often to the distress of the authors of the original books. Papert addresses this issue in his introduction to the second edition of *Mindstorms*.

> I am not sure whether it was my bug or theirs that led academic critics to rush into experiments to prove me wrong in predicting that 'doing Logo' or 'working with computers' would cause change in how children think. I make no such claim anywhere in the book, but I may have made a mistake in waiting until Chapter 8 before saying emphatically that I was not making it. What I was saying, and still say, is something more subtle: I see Logo as a means that can, in principle, be used by educators to support the development of new ways of thinking and learning. However, Logo does not in itself produce good learning any more than paint produces good art.
>
> (Papert, 1993: xiv)

A key benchmark in the development of computer use in UK schools came in 1982/3 when the government provided funds for the purchase of one computer for every primary school. As with so many of the early hardware-based schemes, this was not accompanied by training or significant software access. A further complication at this time, and one which was to continue for many years, was the tripartite computer hardware platform found in UK schools. In order to support British industry, the UK government took the view that it should only support British products. In practice, this meant that Apple computers, especially the Macintosh which had been very popular in US classrooms, could be bought only by schools which found their own funding. Apple computers continue to represent less than 10 per cent of hardware in British schools, although some LEAs, particularly in Scotland, have larger numbers.

This emphasis on the use of in-country products was not unique to the UK. The Tulip computer in the Netherlands was supported in the same way, as were French products in France. In the UK, the main effect of this policy was to delay considerably the point at which many UK schools would move to a hardware platform for which software was widely available.

The first computer to be widely used in UK schools was the BBC B, a hardy and long-lasting computer which had previously been associated mostly with the lone hobbyist. With an emphasis on self-assembly, tinkering and the ability of users to program for it, this was computing at its most amateur but enthusiastic. The Acorn range of computers, based on RISCOS technology, developed from the BBC and were successful until the mid-1990s, when the continuing domination of world IT by Microsoft and the Windows platform finally caused the demise of the company. Xemplar (later Apple Xemplar), a joint venture company, was set up by Apple to maintain the product range and diversify into other hardware. By the end of the decade Xemplar and Apple were much more familiar names than that of Acorn, and Xemplar was selling Windows PCs like everyone else.

The main benefactor of this development in UK education was RM plc, previously Research Machines Ltd. Beginning with the non-standard 380Z and 480Z, the company then produced the Nimbus, an early desktop PC which was not totally IBM-compatible. In the early 1980s it was this company's 380Z which was adopted as standard by influential purchasers such as the Inner London Education Authority. As ILECC's then Technical Support Officer Les Squirrel remembers, these were not cheap machines.

> The price varied between £2000 and £3000, depending on whether the system came with a single and single-sided 5.25" floppy drive, a single double-sided drive or a twin double-sided floppy drive. Monochrome monitors offering green screen displays with 12" screens were supplied. To use the early RGB Cub colour monitors you had to buy an RGB colour circuit board and install it in the 380Z. You used four cables to connect the 380Z to the monitor, at considerable extra cost. Typical RAM size for the 380Z was 16K. If you played with the software, you could steal memory from the graphics card to bring you a massive 47K.
>
> (Les Squirrel, e-mail to the author, 14 March 2000)

The 380Z was not the first RM computer, although it was the first to be widely found in schools. Prior to that, computing enthusiasts such as Peter Andrews were restricted to the earlier models. 'I bought a 280Z; this was just the main processor board, the video board and a keyboard. I provided everything else myself: case, power supply, cassette recorder and the TV set to use as a monitor' (e-mail to the author, 20 March 2000). Andrews purchased this system in June 1978 and the price was £585; a year later he added a twin eight-inch disk drive at an additional cost of £1,398. The mention of a cassette recorder reminds us that this was the first storage system before floppy disks. The earliest 380Z computers had no disk drive and programs were loaded from cassette tape; it could take as long as twelve minutes to do so.

It all seems a lot more than twenty or so years ago and the 380Z/480Z stage of development passed very quickly. With the arrival of the Nimbus, computers in schools began to look more like the machines seen there now. By the late 1980s RM had moved to an industry-standard Windows platform, and with an astute mix of reliability, innovation and listening to customers, it has built itself into a company with a market valuation in 1999 of around a billion pounds.

Supporting the tripartite UK hardware platform was a nightmare too for software developers, especially when the early hobbyists gave way to the later start-up companies, migrating book publishers and innovative thinkers. Those early hobbyists were in many cases the authors of the drill and practice programs that characterised the pioneer years of educational software, and it was only with the development of first Local Education Authority software development, and then the involvement of more expert corporate publishers and developers, that software became more attuned to education's needs, as will be shown.

Even so, it was to be many years before the current awareness of ICT as a set of productivity and creativity tools was to take over from the teacher replacement paradigm beloved of science fiction and uninformed politicians and journalists. This change is in part due to the efforts of the LEA support services in the UK, and in particular to the groups of advisory teachers who supported schools in the 1980s and early 1990s, often carrying their computers with them in order to do so. By the late 1990s the hobbyists were back, with Web publication enabling every teacher – or non-teacher – to set up resource banks, whether altruistically or for profit.

IT and the UK National Curriculum

With the arrival of the first version of the UK National Curriculum in 1988, IT became an integral part of British school life. Since the other nine subjects in the curriculum were very traditional, it surprised many observers when Technology appeared alongside them. An uneasy and doomed marriage of Craft, Design and Technology, Home Economics, Business Education and Computer Education, Technology was to be one of the most difficult subjects in the new curriculum to get right.

There has been much speculation as to how such a revolutionary subject made its way into what was otherwise an unexceptional product of a period of conservatism in politics. It has been suggested by one of those most involved at this stage (Graham, 1993) that there is an 'air of mystery' about how it came to be there. Graham supposes that Kenneth Baker, then Secretary of State at the Department of Education and Science, may well have been involved, since he was the Junior Trade Minister involved in first providing computers for schools. Revealingly, Graham also indicates the initial lack of interest from Her Majesty's Inspectors (HMI) in the topic, a limited understanding that is often discernible in some, although not all, later pronouncements by OFSTED on IT, where the sensible, informed voice of Gabriel Goldstein HMI has not always been the only one to be heard. It is also clear that the success of the TVEI (Technical and Vocational Education Initiative) led ministers to believe that this kind of amalgam of subjects could be beneficial. From that hopeful beginning, the confusions followed.

> it is clear that nobody knew what (technology) was and it was left to the working group to invent it. ... Members of the group began their deliberations without even knowing the title of the course they were considering. ... The only guidance given to the Council was that it was an entirely new subject and was capable of radically changing the way things were taught in schools.
>
> (Graham, 1993: 54)

Further confusion ensued as Art squabbled with Design and Technology for the design area of the curriculum. Eventually Design and Technology was renamed Technology, and Art more clearly encompassed Design, although the picture remains less than totally clear. An even more lively debate developed later around the title to be given to the subject initially called Information Technology.

Among the competing contenders were:

- Information Technology (IT)
- Information and Communications Technology (ICT)
- Information and Communications Technologies (ICT)
- Communication and Information Technologies (C&IT)
- Telematics
- Informatics

The teachers of the subject in question preferred, for the most part, to talk about IT. Users of the technology in other subjects often preferred ICT, especially if their interest revolved around the use of the Internet and other communicative devices. Higher education, always eager to be different, preferred C&IT. Across Europe, telematics seemed to be the preferred term, but the European Community began talking about ICT, and this soon developed a following which was difficult to resist. Niel McLean, then in charge of the subject at the Qualifications and Curriculum Authority (QCA) and later Schools Director at the British Educational Communications and Technology Agency (BECTa), attempted to clarify the matter by suggesting widely that IT described the discrete subject whilst ICT described the use of a set of technologies across the curriculum. This remained the uneasy compromise, until QCA, after McLean's departure, launched the 2000 version of the National Curriculum with the subject renamed ICT. The matter is still unresolved in some minds although ICT is clearly the dominant nomenclature at present.

Further debates related to the role of ICT as a core subject, although not in the National Curriculum sense where the core is formed of English, Mathematics and Science. Many expected ICT to join this grouping, but the emphasis on Literacy and Numeracy Frameworks during the latter part of the 1990s led to some slowing of this process. Many still expect ICT to achieve core status in the future.

The Rise of the Internet

In the introduction to his book on schooling, written in 1970, Illich talks of the need to move away from channelling learners into particular areas and towards what he describes as 'educational webs which heighten the opportunity for each one to transform each moment of his living into one of learning, sharing and caring' (Illich, 1973: 7). It is tempting to see Illich's use of the word 'web' as being remarkably far-sighted, and the World Wide Web, created more than twenty years later, certainly fulfils much of the functionality he describes.

Much of the story of the Internet and education properly belongs in chapter 7, but it is important for now to stress the rapid rise in connectivity in the UK and indeed around the world. The most recent figures, in the BESA Survey, indicate the current state of play (see Table 8).

Table 8   Percentage of schools connected to the Internet 1998–2000

	June 1998	*June 1999*	*April 2000*
Primary	34	58	75
Secondary	87	95	97
Special	N/A	68	84

Source: Savage (1999)

This must represent the fastest and most complete take-up of an entirely new technology in the history of UK education, and certainly deserves extensive discussion. We will return to the Internet in chapter 6.

ICT – a Subject or a Tool?

As has been indicated above, there is an unresolved tension around the issue of ICT as a subject in its own right or as a set of tools with which to deliver and absorb the other subjects of the curriculum. Positions adopted tend to be from the extremes. Those least sympathetic to ICT as a subject tend to see it as the modern-day equivalent of the pen or the printed book, and remind us that although we read books and use pens, we do not (for the most part) study book-binding or the technology of fountain pens. Those who take an opposite stance may see some truth in this argument, but they also argue passionately for the role of ICT – or more often IT – as a subject in its own right that is worthy of study.

In 1989 Derek Esterson, himself the first Inspector for Computer Education in the UK, reported on the state of Computer Studies as a subject within London schools. It was offered as an examination subject by 75 per cent of secondary schools; these exams were taken by almost as many girls as boys, and most courses were linked to Computer Appreciation in the lower secondary years, a term which now seems almost endearingly archaic (Esterson, 1989).

The ILEA – at the instigation of Esterson – insisted on the development of whole-school policies for the use of computers, and this far-sighted decision enabled many London schools more easily to meet the demands for development plans which accompanied later resourcing under the National Grid for Learning at the end of the decade.

The influence of the computer scientists lives on, of course, in terms such as 'computer lab' and in the position of ICT, at least in large secondary schools, as being historically linked to subjects such as Science or Maths, and sharing the resources of the same technician. Esterson noted in 1989 that almost half of the computer education lessons he saw were in computer rooms, but it is likely that the other 50 per cent were for the most part theory lessons rather than involving any great use of computers in ordinary classrooms. The issue continued to interest researchers (Watson, 1990).

The 1999 BESA Survey confirmed the growth in networked computers in UK schools, and indicated the rapid increase in this area in the primary sector. By April 2000, BESA forecast that there would be more than 600,000 networked computers in British schools (see Table 9).

Table 9 Percentage of schools with networked computers 1991–2000

	June 1999	*April 2000*
Primary	37	53
Secondary	95	98
Special	41	52

Source: Savage (1999)

At a time when the UK is seeing a rapid development of computer rooms in primary schools, something piloted in the ILEA in the 1980s but then abandoned in light of the outcomes, it is salutory to note that Papert saw the same thing happen in the USA after the original publication of *Mindstorms*.

> [In *The Children's Machine*] I also describe a trend that became dominant in most schools: moving computers into 'computer labs' where a routinized curriculum of 'computer literacy' would be implemented. Under these conditions, learning often inherited all that was worst in curriculum-driven school practices and learning anything as 'difficult' as 'programming' seemed to be would have gradually withered away – without the second saving circumstance.
>
> (Papert, 1993: xvii)

Papert sees that second important factor to be the development of more powerful forms of LOGO and the accompanying deepening of teacherly understanding of what children are capable of achieving through programming in this language. Papert's model of learning which he describes when discussing LOGO is also extremely appropriate as a description of the kind of incidental but powerful learning that takes place when young people design and create Web sites. Web site publication is a fertile area for understanding current developments, and will be discussed more fully when we return to the subject of the Internet.

> The process reminds one of tinkering; learning consists of building up a set of materials and tools that one can handle and manipulate. Perhaps most central of all, it is a process of working with what you've got.
>
> (Papert, 1993: 173)

The Need for Change

Our schools, as has been shown, have gone through a period of rapid and startling change, both in relation to technology and with regard to the content and delivery of the curriculum. Perhaps this is the most appropriate response to writers such as Postman who have seen schools as resistant to change:

> The institution we call 'school' is what it is because we made it that way. If it is irrelevant, as Marshall McLuhan says; if it shields children from reality, as Norbert Wiener says; if it does not develop intelligence, as Jerome Bruner says; if it is based on fear, as John Holt says; if it avoids the promotion of significant learnings, as Carl Rogers says; if it punishes creativity and independence, as Edgar Friedenberg says; if, in short, it is not doing what needs to be done, it can be changed; it must be changed.
>
> (Postman and Weingartner, 1971: 13)

Schools may have changed, and teachers have certainly had to do so. The job of a UK teacher in 2001 is vastly different from that of a teacher ten or twenty years ago. Has learning changed, however? Do learners interact through the technology now available so that the learning they undertake is differently mediated, managed or assessed? The next chapter will address these issues.

Chapter Summary

- The building we describe as a school is not the only environment in which learning can take place.
- We are seeing increased awareness that learning can be a lifelong activity, making school buildings and methodologies less central to the process.
- Schools have only recently begun to use ICT for productivity rather than practice.
- UK schools are approaching optimum numbers of computers in classrooms.
- Teacher confidence with ICT remains an important issue.
- The issue of ICT as a domain or a set of tools remains unresolved.

Bibliography

DfEE (1998). *Survey of Information and Communications Technology in Schools 1998.* Norwich: The Stationery Office.

—— (1999). *Statistics of Education: Survey of Information and Communications Technology in Schools 1999*, issue no. 13/99. London: The Stationery Office.

Esterson, D. (1989). *Tools for the Mind*. London: Inner London Educational Authority.

Graham, D. (1993). *A Lesson for Us All: The Making of the National Curriculum.* London: Routledge.

Illich, I. (1973). *Deschooling Society*. Harmondsworth: Penguin.

Papert, S. (1993). *Mindstorms: Children, Computers and Powerful Ideas* (2nd edn). New York: Basic Books.

Postman, N. and Weingartner, C. (1971). *Teaching as a Subversive Activity*. London: Penguin.

Savage, D. (ed.) (1999). *ICT in UK State Schools 1999*. London: BESA.

Watson, D. M. (1990). The classroom vs. the computer room. *Computers and Education*, 15(1), 33–7.

4   Learning, Computers and Social Interaction

> Students can look at their grades and even turn in their homework over the Web. Teachers hold online discussion groups. Students e-mail friends and family as naturally as they call them. Students are the ultimate knowledge workers. Their 'job' is to learn and explore and find unexpected relationships between things.
>
> (Gates, 1999: 117)

In this typical vision of the technologically aware school of the present, Microsoft founder Gates reveals a surprising degree of reliance on prior models of learning. The school he describes might be fit for the future, but it still expects homework to be done. The term 'homework' itself is beginning to sound quaint, rooted as it is in a model of schooling which suggests that children should travel each day to a specified geographical location and then reinforce that learning by completing exercises at home in the evening. Teachers are clearly still in charge in Gates's mental model of a school, since they 'hold' online discussion groups rather than participate in them. As others have suggested, teachers do matter and they do make a difference (Rutter, 1979; Vygotsky, 1978).

The notion of students as knowledge workers is an interesting one, designed as it is to fit in to Gates's overall economic argument in his book. Many teachers would feel comfortable with Gates's definition of learning as including the finding of 'unexpected relationships between things' and it is certainly an appropriate description of much learning that is mediated by the use of communication technologies.

As has already been discussed, schools as institutions are changing rapidly as technology alters the paradigm of schooling. In this chapter we consider the changes that have gone on in how we view learning, whether this be through the views of constructivist thinkers, educationists, business economists such as Gates or the thoughts of young learners themselves.

A Young IT Professional Reflects on how he Learns

Nic Lawrence is now an IT support professional, working across Europe for a multinational company and selling his IT knowledge as a freelance consultant. Still only in his early twenties, he left school halfway through the sixth form when employment seemed a more attractive option than more time in education. He reflects here on his first experiences with computers, and the extent to which the IT he learnt at school has been of any relevance to him in the work he does now.

> I first remember coming across a computer around 1989, in hospital for some reason or other, it was a BBC Micro. I remember it was like a cool video game on a trolley, and I hadn't a clue how to do to anything on it ... so I didn't. It actually scared me.

> The first computer I owned was one of those little Noddy ones, like a Sinclair Spectrum; it wasn't a Sinclair, and it wasn't as good, but you get the idea. That was when I was in the last few years of primary school. It was a case of 'Read the manual from front to cover – not understand any of it and type in the example programs to see what beeps and colours it could do and stuff'. In school at that time it was all BBC Micros, and because they were still a pretty new thing to have, only the teachers loaded anything up on them. We just followed the on-screen instructions. So up until then I didn't have any real computer knowledge to speak of.

> During secondary school it was a big jump up to 286 PCs running Windows 3.x. That's when I really started to get into computers with a passion. This was not so much from learning how to add up cells in Excel from IT lessons at school, (something that I knew inside out then, but eludes me now although I wish I could remember it for my tax returns) but from the 'My computer is better than your computer' argument with other students. I had an Atari 520STfm (I can remember the exact model), which used to have battles with the Commodore Amiga crowd which were not dissimilar to those between the PC and Apple Mac fans today.

> Back then there were numerous computing magazines available for both the Atari and Amigas, offering not only freebie games but little operating system utilities and the like. Both computers were aimed at home gaming (remember that the traditional gaming consoles were still in their early years then): you could still get involved in how they actually worked, and learn something useful about computers in

general which would actually hold you in good stead for under-standing IT and computing in general in the future.

In the third or fourth year at secondary school I sold my Atari (a very emotional time – I even had my photo taken with it before I sold it), and I got a little 386 PC for Christmas. That was really it for me. DOS just gave you so many possibilities to fiddle, and there was still a nice range of magazines for the novice to learn from. Originally, when I found a modem and got connected to the CompuServe Information Service (CIS), it really was just using the modem for mail, and for meeting people online After a while I had to pack that in because of the phone bills. I set up my own Bulletin Board System (BBS). The BBS really taught me a lot. There really was a whole community around BBSing, very much like regular IRC (Internet Relay Chat) users today. You found that people who started BBSs back then were split into two distinct groups, just like those that run a BOT (robot software) on IRC or write their own webpages today; the serious fanatic and the poor newbie who is destined to be ridiculed and have their work destroyed by others.

There was just so much I learnt from the BBS. How the cheapest modems were the most reliable, network security to keep the hackers out from shredding my hard drives, local networking to get diskless workstations working as a second dial-up node, user-interface design and ANSI graphics were just a few of them. The big driving force to try and learn more and more to make your BBS bigger and better was a kind of one-upmanship to get more active users on your BBS and more calls from users per day than any other BBS sysop (system operator).

I remember I once set up a little collaborative group of BBS sysops who would share their user base, share their filesystem and netmail [netmail is the BBS equivalent of Usenet]. That was pretty interes-ting. It's a shame that BBS are now all but dead because they really did offer focused use and content, which were truly 100% secure and customer-focused. Most of them were free too, and without the slow response time you have on the Net.

When the BBSs were dead because of the evil Net taking away all our customers, I more or less got into the Web purely for e-mail, surfing a bit and for company e-mail. Still up the point when I left school and got my first job I didn't have an awful lot of Internet know-how. I had a basic grounding in the topic, which was more than a lot of people had, but I've never considered myself to really know about something until I can literally or metaphorically take it apart and put it back together again.

Of course when I got my first job I said I wanted to learn more about networking and not do any programming. I immediately started to learn how to program, and didn't do anything to do with networking or hardware. So while they were training me up in programming, (which I'm now very grateful they did), I started playing around with the Internet in my own time, with a half hearted attempt to rebuild my old BBS on the web. This was hopeless as I only now just have enough know-how to do such a project.

Strangely enough, when I started to learn to program at work, although I was undoubted the worst programmer in the company, I had far more knowledge of how PCs actually worked. Half the programmers couldn't work Windows properly, and as soon as there was a slight problem with any PC hardware, or Word crashing or something, they'd come running to me. I can only think that that's because I started off on the Atari and an empty 386 where there were no applications to go wrong, so the only thing to learn and master was the computer itself. I think that when most people learn about computers, they learn in reverse. Typically they learn first about applications, and only then about the computer and operating system: or perhaps only the applications. It's like learning how to run before you can walk.

So from there I pretty much learnt a small handful of languages, and in my own time had some fun with the Internet. I had only really mastered two areas of computers up to then, BBSing and DOS. I think I really learnt a lot when I left my first job and worked freelance for 10 months. There are several reasons for this: I had lots more time to practise and perfect my programming skills; I didn't want to be left behind in the industry with no marketable skills, so I made a conscious effort to learn at least one new and useful programming language (PERL); and I had less to worry about.

I joined a new company. Improving my existing programming skills that I was selling to customers was a breeze. I was at last able to use my customers as a testing bed for new and interesting programming techniques, where before I couldn't for my last employer as every minute of my time had to be accounted for, and there were always tight schedules to be kept. This was great. Not only did it mean I felt good about the work I was doing, but it made me a master at what I was doing, and eventually got me the job I'm doing today, which I love.

> There's only one way to learn a new programming language cheaply and quickly, and it doesn't involve expensive training courses. I bought as many O'Reilly Associates books as I could find on Perl, and started a big project to put it to use on. So one day when I was bored I started my current website, logged on to IRC, and asked lots of stupid questions of the real gurus. I got kicked and banned from several channels. I wrote some more code. I copied some code. I asked some more questions, and I am eventually, slowly, becoming one of the regulars and accepted non-idiots in Perl on a few IRC networks. My current website is very much like the BBS. Firstly it's something to focus my time and creative attention to. It's a real challenge, and in some senses something that I can show off to other people.
>
> (Nic Lawrence, e-mail to the author, 9 Feb 2000)

As Lawrence makes clear, there are many more appropriate settings for learning than some of our classrooms. His experience as a learner in formal settings was not very productive and he left school early, even though the comprehensive school he attended was known for its extensive use of technology. His technical expertise, which was already extensive by his mid-teens, ensured that he was able to gain highly paid employment in the IT industry. He now travels Europe solving database problems for clients, and is still only in his early twenties.

Lawrence has used manuals only to learn programming languages, and has learnt about ICT only rarely from direct instruction by a teacher or lecturer. Instead, he has used the communicative possibilities of his own Bulletin Board System and later the Internet to contact others, not always young people, who were attempting to solve similar problems. By working together, these virtual groupings are able to assemble and synthesise group knowledge, and share understandings.

For Nic, learning is not about the transmission of knowledge or the remembering of facts; it is crucially related to learning from others, and being able to reconstruct what has previously been taken apart to be understood. As he says, 'I've never considered myself to really know about something until I can literally or metaphorically take it apart and put it back together again'.

Papert and LOGO – Alternatives to Drill and Practice

Early computer software was based on a behaviourist view of learning. The programmers of that drill and practice software assumed that learning would take place if correct responses were rewarded and incorrect ones received no reward. As will be shown in the next chapter, such ideas have been very persistent in the world of educational software, and can be seen still in the Integrated Learning Systems of the 1990s.

Very few educational computing programs have been based on alternative theories of learning, although many software tools have been used within learning environments informed by these theories. A particular focus for the development of software linked to constructivist theories of learning has been the Massachusetts Institute of Technology (MIT) and in particular the work there of Seymour Papert and his research associates. Papert's development of the computer program LOGO is a significant step in the development of educational software, for it is based on clearly held theories of learning, rather than on the simplistic assumptions regarding rote learning which underpin the work of many other programmers.

Papert has written about the development of LOGO (Papert, 1980) and the extent to which it has been used as he expected (Papert, 1996). His starting point was his belief that computers were being used to program children, and that it would be much more effective for learning if it were the children programming the computers. Papert acknowledges his debt to Piaget, on whose knowledge-based theory of learning many of his ideas are based. Papert attempts to reinterpret Piagetian thinking in the light of the availability of computers, and this leads him to consider one aspect of computer theory: Artificial Intelligence, often shortened to AI.

> The definition of artificial intelligence can be narrow or broad. In the narrow sense, AI is concerned with extending the capacity of machines to perform functions that would be considered intelligent if performed by people. Its goal is to construct machines and, in doing so, it can be thought of as a branch of advanced engineering. But in order to construct such machines, it is usually necessary to reflect not only on the nature of machines but on the nature of the intelligent functions to be performed.
>
> (Papert, 1980: 157)

Papert continues this argument by explaining the close link between language and learning, and the way in which LOGO was designed to build on this. He reminds his readers of the links between AI on the one hand, and linguistics and psychology on the other. He also explains Piagetian understandings of learning as being at least as much concerned with the nature of the knowledge as with the learning process. 'To understand how a child learns number', Papert suggests, 'we have to study number' (Papert, 1980: 158). The example he gives to explain this further is that of riding a bicycle. Investigating the attributes of the rider might, he explains, be interesting; but it would be irrelevant to the task of learning to ride the bicycle. That task is possible because of the laws of physical motion which govern the efficacy of bicycles; if the bicycle is incorrectly designed then no learner can ride it.

Activity

In most contemporary educational situations where children come into contact with computers the computer is used to put children through their paces, to provide exercises of an appropriate level of difficulty, to provide feedback, and to dispense information. The computer programming the child. In the LOGO environment the relationship is reversed: The child, even at pre-school ages, is in control: The child programs the computer. And in teaching the computer how to think, children embark on an exploration about how they themselves think. The experience can be heady: Thinking about thinking turns the child into an epistemologist, an experience not even shared by most adults.

(Papert, 1980: 19)

- Does this match your own experience of the use of LOGO in schools? If not, why not?
- Many would suggest that LOGO has been used in many classrooms in a way which is quite the reverse of that suggested by Papert; why do you think this might have happened?

Papert explains that it was his background in mathematics and psychology that led him to be interested in the use of computers to help people think, in particular the 'acquisition of spatial thinking and the ability to deal with size and quantity' (Papert, 1980: 166). This is an appropriate explanation of the activities that many learners have undertaken with Papert's LOGO programming language. Papert had been thinking about a programming language suitable for children since the 1960s and later developed LOGO, in collaboration with others, at MIT Boston's Artificial Intelligence Laboratory.

LOGO attracted a great deal of interest around the world, especially in the 1980s when computers capable of running it become common in classrooms in much of Europe and North America. Enthusiasts seized upon the program as offering something quite different from the drill software which was otherwise the dominant mode. And yet, twenty years later, LOGO seems much less of a force than it once was, despite its easy availability and the mentions it gets in many curricular documents, including the UK Maths Curriculum. In the end, it may have been the identification of Maths with LOGO that was the biggest problem. Papert recognises that LOGO had much to do with his background in Mathematics but he always intended it to be used in a much wider sense. In classrooms, however, LOGO has been more often used to draw geometric shapes than it has to design branching stories. In many ways the floor robots, which have maintained a presence, offer a present-day version of the LOGO experience, with the early cable-connected turtle replaced by such later devices as, in the UK, the Valiant Roamer and the Swallow Systems Pip and Pixie.

Papert continues to consider the impact of computers on learning, however, and he sees the time when schools must change, predicted by him twenty years ago, as now being imminent. Writing in 1980 about his concept of a learning society, Papert noted the obstacles that exist when we try to think of a world without schools, most of them related to the experience we have each had of such a system. Papert called then for alternatives to schools which would not be an absence of schooling but 'elaborated models of the nonschool activities in which children would engage' (Papert, 1980: 178).

Papert has more recently addressed the issue of schooling in a book which looks at the impact that computers in the home are having on learning processes (Papert, 1996). In this book, aimed at parents and the general reader, Papert makes little mention of school or schooling but concentrates instead on the learning that takes place between and around children and computers. He contrasts what he sees as the two approaches taken by the designers of computer and video games: the instructionist and the constructionist. The instructionist – the current version of the drill and practice designer – he describes as 'school-style learning in the context of a game. ... The machine asks a question. The kid responds. The machine creates a threat in the game. The kid responds. By some sleight of language this is called interactive ...' (Papert, 1996: 47–8). Constructionist designers, on the other hand, would prefer that the child designed the game.

It is interesting to note the use here of constructionism rather than the more usual constructivism. Constructivist learning theory, rooted in the theories of Vygotsky (Vygotsky, 1962, 1978) and much discussed over the last twenty years, has been very influential among the academic world but has yet to affect to any great extent some instruments of education such as the UK National Curriculum or general mainstream British teacherly practice.

Papert and his collaborator Idit Harel have written (Papert and Harel, 1991) of constructionism as the dominant ideology associated with the Epistemology and Learning Research Group at MIT. As in his earlier writing, Papert tends to situate constructionism here as in opposition to instructionism, but he is at pains to stress that this is not to criticise the latter, but should rather serve to indicate the difference. One example he gives is from the world of mathematics teaching:

I do not mean to imply that constructionists see instruction as bad. That would be silly. The question at issue is on a different level: I am asking what kinds of innovation are liable to produce radical change in how children learn. ... It is obvious that instruction in mathematics is on the average very poor. But it does not follow that the route to better performance is necessarily the invention by researchers of more powerful and effective means of instruction (with or without computers).

The diffusion of cybernetic construction kits into the lives of children could in principle change the context of the learning of mathematics. Children might come to want to learn it because they would use it in building these models ...

(Papert and Harel, 1991: 7)

A growing awareness of the importance of home learning is apparent in the 1991 volume, but it is more fully developed in Papert's most recent book, which deals with the technologically connected family. It is to the home that we must look in order to understand some of the far-reaching changes that have taken place in the availability to young people of alternative methods of learning.

Learning in the Home

One outcome of the 1960s and 1970s, particularly in the USA, has been an increase in the numbers of children who are educated at home, usually by parents. The home-schooling movement may have had its roots in the hippie generation and the communal lifestyle, but it has become a socially acceptable choice within some social groupings, especially for those who are relatively affluent and can therefore devote the necessary time to the task.

Much of the criticism of home-schooling has referred not to any diminution of educative possibilities where parents are the teachers but to a general concern about the lack of social interaction for the child, even in the largest of families. The Internet has come as a boon to the movement, offering as it does the possibility for interaction between the home-schooled children of all those families involved. It provides also the crucial support and approval needed by parents who have made the momentous decision to take their children out of the school system.

By early 2000, the home-schooling movement was big enough to support a number of magazines and other resources, including Home Education (http://www.home-ed-press.com/wlcm_HEM.html), which had been in existence since 1983. In the February 2000 issue of the magazine, parent Teri Brown described going with her daughter to meet a friend she had made online. As Brown recognises, this could be a dangerous course to take, but she describes the precautions that were necessary. She also notes the extent to which online support has changed the face of home-schooling:

> To those outside the cyber world of online support what we were doing was strange at best, dangerous at worst. But to the hundreds of thousands of us who chat, encourage, love, and cry with one another via the Internet it was a normal phenomenon. I was surprised how many homeschoolers I met online have gone out of their way to meet other homeschooling moms in real life.
>
> I don't think it would be an overstatement to say that the cyber world is changing the face of homeschooling. Between chatrooms and support lists, people from different parts of the country are getting to know one another. These people may have different faiths, different philosophies of education, and different interests, but they all have one thing in common. They and their children have embarked on the wonderful, amazing journey that is homeschooling
>
> (Brown, 2000)

The Home Education magazine Web site lists an extensive list of online resources to advise on everything from correspondence programmes to laws and regulations (http://www.home-ed-magazine.com/HSRSC/hsrsc_gn.html). The Canadian Alliance of Home Schoolers was formed in 1979 and now estimates that 30,000 families are educating their children at home in that country (http://www.life.ca/hs/). Many home-schooling sites act as advertisements for their authors' books as well as meeting places for participants. This is true of Home School Zone (http://www.homeschoolzone.com/main.htm), which also has an extensive series of links to activities in many different countries.

The UK site lists two organisations: Education Otherwise (http://www.education-otherwise.org/), formed in 1977, and the much newer Home Education Advisory Service (http://www.heas.org.uk/), launched in 1999, presumably in response to an increased size in the market for such an offering. Both agencies sell a number of booklets and offer advice and a subscription service for parents.

The aims of Education Otherwise are to:

- Encourage learning outside the school system.
- Re-affirm that parents have the primary responsibility for their children's education and that they have the right to exercise this responsibility by educating them out of school.
- Establish the primary right of children to have full consideration given to their wishes and feelings about their education.

(http://www.education-otherwise.org/eo%20site%20stuff/aims.htm
[4 February 2000])

Even in homes where children have continued to attend school in a traditional way, the effects of technology have often been noted by parents, especially where they may themselves have a developed understanding of what is taking place. This is certainly true of Linda Spear, a parent who is also a senior IT adviser in Cambridgeshire. Aware of the potential of technology, she shares her observations here of her son's growing understanding and sophisticated use of technologies unknown to previous generations. She begins by describing his easy confidence with the paramount communicative technology of his generation: the mobile phone.

My youngest son is part of a sibling group of three and one of the things I notice about their behaviour is how easily they communicate with each other using text messaging on their mobile phones. I felt excluded and wanted to join in as I watched how they switched on the text messaging option, and I sat transfixed by their dexterity in tapping in text. Soon I did it too: it was faster than e-mail, more personal and very inclusive. This technology is touching many more lives than personal computers but still some will miss out.

I notice because as a teacher – and now a trainer – I can't help doing so. I noticed how easily my son slips between tools for communicating and working. He uses saws and drills for his A level projects and online forums to share his innermost thoughts with people who he thinks are like him. He manages websites of varying complexity for universities half way across the world on subjects new and exciting such as robotics.

So who taught him? The answer is clear – he learned from what he had around him, and found, and was offered to work with. His school provides a solid dependable traditional curriculum, where undoubtedly the discipline of working to a model of examinations will allow him to move into a sector of society such as a university that will provide him with further opportunity to widen that way of working so that he will have the opportunity of a job or research post.

The really exciting discovery of tussling with a problem until he found a solution, or testing a theory, came from outside that environment. He and his friends accept that school will not provide all the challenges they need to grow intellectually. My son's thinking processes are sophisticated beyond his real level of experience. Yet he is still a young person growing up, and complicated and adolescent feelings still lead his life.

We realised early on this particular child had a talent for thinking long and hard about learning and he could generalise at a young age. His play tools were not nice tidy Lego sets which made kits but lots of mixed up pieces of Lego and other materials to imagine with. He was encouraged to 'jump the hoops' at his primary school and in return we provided him with computers and electronic gadgets that entranced and engaged him.

He thinks about scientific and mathematical ideas as if they were everyday, not because he is gifted or even talented, though as his mother I am sure he is all of these! It is because the opportunity to develop and focus on a real passion and interest was encouraged and funded by his parents. His own time was his contribution.

So how did we know that he would not waste the resources he was given? We didn't: we took the view that he would pick things up, work with them, seek help and support when he wanted it and would leave it when he needed to think about something else. He often came back to something abandoned months before.

His room is a tip. To him and his friends its a place where they construct and build and make. The computer for them is another construction kit and talking with other people who are also constructors, whether of physical things such as robots, or of ideas, is normal to him. Interestingly, each of his close friends is similar to him but has completely different talents, whether these be in art or music. None of them is awed by the other's talents; they are totally relaxed about the fact that they have something school doesn't provide: a sense of identity.
(Linda Spear, e-mail to the author, 9 Febraruy 2000)

Spear's comments show not just the depth of her awareness of her son's learning and her understanding of the potential of technology to meet adolescent needs, but also her developed perception of the changes that are happening in young people's lives as a result of their appropriation of technologies that offer something to them.

Her son uses the Short Message Service (SMS) on his mobile phone not because someone sold him the idea through advertising or because he has been told to do so; he uses it because it meets his personal and very typically adolescent need for easy and private communication with his peers. Crucially, technology is for him all about true interaction; he has nothing in common with the reductive and inaccurate stereotype of the adolescent 'mouse potato', slumped passively in front of his computer screen. That stereotype has far more validity for the incomplete assumption of these technologies by older generations than it does for the young people for whom such devices have always been available.

There is an interesting example here of the role of parents in the educative process. Spear's decision to fund her son's interests is the enlightened decision of a thoughtful educationist, and has little in common with the parent who buys a computer because advertising has suggested it will be advantageous. Such decisions do not come cheap but they do hold up a pattern of education in which the school as a site for learning is just one of several contexts that are relevant. As Illich reminds us, 'We have all learned most of what we know outside school. Pupils do most of their learning without, and often despite, their teachers' (Illich, 1973: 35).

Papert knows this too, but sees the school as an intermediate stage surrounded by learning experiences which may be more meaningful and long-lasting (Papert, 1996). He describes the young child's experience of 'home-style learning' as being 'self-directed, experiential, (and) non-verbal'. There then follows a period of 'school-style learning', where the child can no longer learn unless 'adults are willing to explain or teach'. Finally, the child escapes school-style learning, and 'the pursuit of knowledge is once more under the learner's control' (Papert, 1996: 193).

This is a persuasive, neat and convincing model, although not one which is generally accepted. It begs many questions, not least the assumption that school is one experience rather than many: the child attending a large inner-city comprehensive has nothing like the same experience of school as her counterpart attending a private residential school. Even such unconventional establishments as Summerhill School still carry the label 'school', but what happens in them may be nearer to Papert's home-style learning.

In his most recent book Papert gives most of his attention to what is happening in the home, a household which he suggests contains a connected family which needs to bridge what he characterises as a digital generation gap (Papert, 1996). Concerning himself with a group of young people who have been described as the N-Gen (Tapscott, 1998) – the Net Generation – his basic thesis revolves around the implications of the 'love affair' he perceives between children and computers, a state of affairs he claims to have seen in many different parts of the world.

> Everywhere, with very few exceptions, I see the same gleam in their eyes, the same desire to appropriate this thing. And more than wanting it, they seem to know that in a deep way it already belongs to

them. They know they can master it more easily and more naturally than their parents. They know they are the computer generation.

(Papert, 1996: 1)

It is precisely romanticism of this order that has tended to diminish Papert in the eyes of some of his critics. Seen as a futurologist and populist by some, he has often been unfairly criticised by those who have read only his more popular texts. *The Connected Family* (1996), from which the quotation above is taken, is not an overly academic book but one aimed at parents, and it is the less widely known books such as *Constructionism* (1991) which contain the fully elaborated arguments appropriate for academic circles. *The Connected Family* is also an indication of the consistency of Papert's arguments; the points he makes here are only contemporary re-phrasings of those he has been making ever since the publication of *Mindstorms* (1980). Of course, technology has moved on since *Mindstorms*, and *The Connected Family* comes with an accompanying CDROM and a linked Web site (http://www.connectedfamily.com/).

Considering learning from a parental point of view, Papert suggests that Western shopping malls offer parents two conflicting views of learning: the quiet non-technological status-laden bookshop and the CDROM-aware technological toy or computer shop. When he looks at what is available as educational software, Papert sees too often an impoverished version of what might be possible, based on flawed or incomplete theories of learning and an increasingly rapid return to an environment dominated by rote and drills. The images may be more complex, animated or video-enhanced, but the activities are too often those which were largely rejected by educationists up to twenty years ago.

Parents, of course, are a new and much larger group to sell to, and it is clear that it is some ill-defined notion of educational value and support that persuades many parents to spend large sums of money on a computer for their children. Having spent the money, they may not notice that for much of the time it is not the CDROM encyclopaedia that is being used but a flight simulator, or that the Internet connection is used not as an online library but in order to play *Quake* and other Internet-enhanced games with young people around the world.

Papert goes on to outline to parents the oppositional modes of computer use that have concerned him for many years, although the instructionist–constructionist axis is here modified to that of behaviourism or constructivism. He does not, however, suggest that one is good and the other bad, rather that both kinds of learning are real but that there needs to be a balance between them. Educational software has always relied heavily on behaviourist understandings of learning, and so have many schools; and Papert is less than convinced that school is an appropriate site for learning, at least in its North American form.

Schools may have changed, he suggests, but only to a degree. He notes that the use of word processors has become uniform and unmarked, but suggests that it would be insupportable for anything else to be the case. Bigger change, the 'megachange' he hopes for, is quite different.

Activity

Of course I do not suggest that we run out waving banners and demanding megachange tomorrow. Microchange is meant to represent the end of the scale that should be implemented now. Megachange is meant to represent an ideal that gives direction to smaller changes we can strive for right away.

(Papert, 1996: 157)

- What microchanges have you seen (in relation to ICT) during your teaching career?
- Your school's ICT Development Plan could be said to be a plan for megachange – is it? If not, why are Development Plans not used in this way?

Papert uses the privileges of age and experience to paint a picture of upswings and downswings in technology use in schools. His interpretation can be summarised as:

- Early 1960s: first great enthusiasm.
- 1970s: enthusiasm subsides – then microcomputers create bigger romantic visions.
- Early 1980s: expressive use of computers dominant in the few schools that have them.
- 1980s: use of computers becomes routine and traditional in nature.
- 1990s: next romantic period related to the Internet and cyberspace.

(Summarised from Papert, 1996: 161)

This is a persuasive model and certainly holds good within a British context. The first great enthusiasm arrived here a little later than in the USA, and was mostly linked to the home computing and programming possibilities of the BBC computer; but it was certainly a romantic period in the widest sense of the word. Early school uses of the microcomputer were often both expressive and essentially arts-based. Word processing quickly became a key activity, but at that time it was more likely to be seen as a creative as well as a productive tool. Desktop publishing programs, now almost totally superseded by the extensive tools in current word processors, offered a range of possibilities which related to changing the look of the text. The first programs which offered a choice of fonts for printing were very influential; although teachers of English may have felt they took pupils away from communicating meaning in words, they certainly opened up the possibilities of sharing meaning through image, colour and form.

Later in the 1980s computer use became much more routine in the UK and the drill and practice programs gained supremacy, an achievement which they have largely maintained. The first real threat to these reductive activities with computers has been the romantic flowering of cyberspace with all its associated misunderstandings, hopelessly overstated hype and ecstatic gurglings.

Learning through Collaboration: The Role of Technology

For many educationists, a key to the real potential of the computer lies in its ability to promote collaboration. This may be of the most immediate kind, with two or three children working together to compose a text, or it may be much more complex with the same young people making use of online contacts to discuss, reformulate, test models and learn from others.

The greater availability of the Internet has offered new mechanisms for these activities. Synchronous communication, in particular, has been seized upon by young people who are hungry for communication but may be challenged by coping with the concepts they want to discuss in more traditional settings. Synchronous communication on the Internet originally developed through the use of Internet Relay Chat (IRC), a Finnish invention which allows two or more people, connected to the Internet at the same time, to exchange text, graphics and sound with each other. More recently, online chat on the Web has made this facility even more widely available, and it has been suggested (Spender, 1995) that this has been at least partly responsible for the rapid rise in the numbers of women and girls who are online.

Asynchronous communication has a much longer history since it is technologically less demanding, although intellectually very challenging for those who use it. First available in the form of newsgroups (Usenet) and Bulletin Board Systems (BBS), asynchronous communication is now usually to be found in the Web forums which multiplied at the end of the 1990s, examples including Yahoo Clubs, Microsoft Communities, Onelist mailing lists and many others. Maintaining the line or argument in an asynchronous communication is extremely difficult; it is for this reason that so much of what is said is both bad-tempered and irritable. Contributors misunderstand or breach conventions, answer a message without noticing that this has already been done, or commit the worst breach of 'Netiquette' by sending a personal reply to a whole online community.

It is within adult asynchronous communications, however, that this degree of irritation and unskilled use is most pronounced. Among younger and more expert users there is often greater tolerance and a considerably more developed understanding of the process, which itself leads to fewer errors. Asynchronous communication has also been formalised within the educational system by the adoption of tools such as First Class, Learning Space and WebCT. All of these commercial tools aim to harness both synchronous and asynchronous communication and manage it within the traditional setting of a course at a particular institution. These tools can be used to replace a course with a distance education model, or to provide online support for a course which also involves face-to-face contact.

Unfortunately, as research has shown (Watson *et al.*, 1998), learners within formal educational settings, especially those who are not technologically expert or who do not have ready access to an adequate level of resources, will not use these tools as their online instructors had hoped they would do. Much work remains to be done before educators learn how to use synchronous and asynchronous communication effectively within formal learning structures.

Illich foresaw the use of computers to create communities of learners. Writing about the need for skills exchanges, learning situations in which people learn from each other rather than playing the roles of teacher and taught, he envisages computer uses which are now totally routine:

> The operation of a peer-matching network would be simple. The user would identify himself by name and address and describe the activity for which he sought a peer. A computer would send him back the names and addresses of all those who had inserted the same description. It is amazing that such a simple utility has never been used on a broad scale for publicly valued activity.
>
> In its most rudimentary form, communication between client and computer could be established by return mail. In big cities typewriter terminals could provide instantaneous responses. The only way to retrieve a name and address from the computer would be to list an activity for which a peer was sought. People using the system would become known only to their potential peers.
>
> A complement to the computer could be a network of bulletin boards and classified newspaper ads, listing the activities for which the computer could not produce a match. No names would have to be given. Interested readers would then introduce their names into the system. A publicly supported peer-match network might be the only way to guarantee the right of free assembly and to train people in the exercise of this most fundamental civic activity.
>
> (Illich, 1973: 95)

With computers now able to accomplish even more than Illich foresaw, it is striking to note that his vision, of a 'publicly supported peer-match network' is an apt description of some of the most popular uses of the World Wide Web. He even uses the analogy of a web when looking forward to alternatives to the present system, when he states that 'the alternative to scholastic funnels is a world made transparent by true communication webs' (Illich, 1973: 105).

Does the Learner Need a Teacher?

No discussion of the role of the learner can avoid grappling with that of the teacher, and the extent to which teaching and learning may or may not be connected. Like learners, teachers can operate in many different models, each with their own motivations, desires and beliefs. One way of distinguishing between different teacherly styles is to consider the mental models each teacher appears to be using (Postman and Weingartner, 1971; Marshall, 2000).

> For example, there is the teacher who believes he is in the lighting business. We may call him the Lamplighter. When he is asked what he is trying to do with his students, his reply is something like this: 'I want to illuminate their minds, to allow some light to penetrate the darkness'. Then there is the Gardener. He says, 'I want to cultivate their minds, to fertilise them, so that the seeds I plant will flourish'. There is also the Personnel Manager, who wants nothing more than to keep his students' minds busy, to make them efficient and industrious. The Muscle Builder wants to strengthen flabby minds, and the Bucket Filler wants to fill them up.
>
> (Postman and Weingartner, 1971: 86)

It is clear that some of these kinds of teacher will be more likely to use technology in their teaching than others. The Lamplighter may well resent the technology since it appears to usurp the teacher's role as the illuminating agent. Some technologies may hold more interest for him, however, particularly those, such as the electronic whiteboard, which maintain the focus of the class on the teacher. The Gardener may feel a little less threatened by technology, although not if the spurs to growth are produced by understandings gleaned online rather than from a teacher-mentor. The Personnel Manager who wants to keep students busy will be delighted with some aspects of computer technology, such as Integrated Learning Systems, but is likely to be particularly suspicious of uses which seem to involve lengthy thought as opposed to action. The Muscle Builder wants to find suitable training material online, and the Bucket Filler will have no problem finding large amounts of content, but even they are unlikely to see technology as anything other than ancillary to their purpose.

It is to another model of teacherly practice that we must turn if we are to see a way forward for teachers alongside technology. Much talk in recent years has revolved around the extent to which constructivist theories of learning have resulted in a new paradigm of the teacher as mentor rather than instructor, working alongside students rather than leading from the front. This fits neatly with the experience of many teachers: when I first had a computer in my classroom I was struck by the frequency with which I found myself working alongside my students rather than with them facing me. It would be easy to overstate this change of course, and it may be that some at least of the change was cosmetic and merely resulted from the physical location of teacher and learner both facing the technology, but many would suggest that the changes begun then have had fundamental effects on teacher–student relationships. My later employment of Web site designers still in their teens to build university research Web sites was in many ways the logical outcome of the experience of genuinely working alongside my students in the early days of computers in classrooms.

Chapter Summary

- Although behaviourist models of learning are still influential in software design, they are increasingly challenged in the wider educational sphere by varied forms of constructivist, socially-mediated models of learning.
- Young people have often been much quicker to embrace and make sensible use of new technologies than have the educational institutions they attend.
- Papert's model of the phases through which educational uses of computers has progressed is a useful mechanism by which to consider the different uses that might be possible.
- Much that appears interactive in educational software may in fact be very traditional in its reliance on rote learning and drill and practice.
- The recent history of educational software development can be seen in terms of behaviourist vs constructivist models of learning.
- Technology has supported and accelerated the development of alternative models of schooling which are based in the home.
- Technology is not the threat or mystery to the young people of today that it will always be, at least in part, to their parents.
- The future for the technology-assisted teacher is within a modified form of the traditional role, emphasising mentoring and guidance over leadership and instruction.

Bibliography

Brown, T. (2000). *Electronic Homeschooling Support: A Warmly Human Endeavor.* *Home Education Magazine*, Jan.–Feb. Available: http://www.home-ed-press.com/HEM/171.00/jf_art_endv.html [4 February 2000].

Gates, B. (1999). *Business Using a Digital Nervous System.* London: Penguin.

Illich, I. (1973). *Deschooling Society.* Harmondsworth: Penguin.

Marshall, B. (2000). A rough guide to English teachers. *English in Education*, 34, 24–41.

Papert, S. (1980). *Mindstorms: Children, Computers and Powerful Ideas.* New York: Basic Books.

—— (1996). *The Connected Family: Bridging the Generation Gap.* Atlanta, GA: Longstreet Press.

Papert, S. and Harel, I. (eds). (1991). *Constructionism.* Norwood, NJ: Ablex Publishing.

Postman, N. and Weingartner, C. (1971). *Teaching as a Subversive Activity.* London: Penguin.

Rutter, M. (1979). *Fifteen Thousand Hours: Secondary Schools and their Effects on Children.* London: Open Books.

Spender, D. (1995). *Nattering on the Net: Women, Power and Cyberspace.* Melbourne: Spinifex Press.

Tapscott, D. (1998). *Growing up Digital: The Rise of the Net Generation.* New York: McGraw-Hill.

Vygotsky, L. (1962). *Thought and Language.* Boston: The MIT Press.

—— (1978). *Mind in Society.* Cambridge, MA: The MIT Press.

Watson, D., Blakeley, B. and Abbott, C. (1998). Researching the use of communication technologies in teacher education. *Computers and Education*, 30(1–2), 15–21.

5   Educational Responses to Technology

Most educational systems do not respond quickly to technological advances. Schools, colleges and universities are, by their very nature, conservators of prior knowledge, accepted understandings and proven methodologies. The teacher who has learnt using one technology is not likely to move readily to others unless clear and irrefutable evidence is provided of the efficacy of doing so.

It is easy to forget how much change has been seen in learning technologies by the current generation of teachers. By no means at the end of my career now, I am nevertheless old enough to be able to stun my current student teachers by describing my use of what we called a 'dip-in pen' at my inkwell-equipped desk at Devizes Road Primary School in Wiltshire in the 1950s and 1960s. Ballpoint pens were forbidden by many teachers then, since it was thought that they encouraged sloppy writing. Felt-tip pens had been invented – just – and I well remember that my infant teacher had one: a mysterious-smelling sleek black object it was too, in a velvet-lined case. It was used on special occasions only, usually to make flash cards for reading.

By my grammar school years, technology, for students at least, had moved only as far as the fountain pen: an interesting demonstration of the power of levers and pumps for physicists, but an ever-present potential for disaster in the pockets of a schoolboy. The sudden arrival of the cartridge-loading pen created considerable excitement, but not as much as there would be a little later when the school was told at assembly that we were moving into the future since teaching machines would be arriving.

Technology before Computers – the Short Reign of the Teaching Machine

The short and disappointing history of the teaching machine is worthy of more attention than can be given to it here. Thought of as the latest technology in the early 1960s, teaching machines were in fact no more than microfiche readers full of multiple choice questions, often related to

68

aspects of the mathematics or physics curriculum. At Bishop Wordsworth Grammar School they were proudly installed in a science laboratory, taking up much of the space previously available for experiments, and we duly set to work with great excitement. Unfortunately, the excitement lasted for little more than a lesson or two, and the activity soon became extremely tedious. What happened to the machines was not vouchsafed to this unimportant schoolboy, but they may languish still in some far cupboard, ready to be unearthed for a museum display in the future.

We are reminded here of what has been sometimes described as the pendulum of educational innovation, which seems to swing from one extreme to the other and never stops in the middle. Attributing this paradigm to one of the professors who taught her, Mellon (1999) also notes that it is often the 'technology zealots' who start the pendulum swinging. Mellon's technology zealots may of course be Papert's teacher enthusiasts, and the differing terminology each author uses says much about their respective beliefs. Mellon, although herself a Professor in an Educational Technology department, is convinced of the centrality of the teacher, whatever other resources may be available: 'Technology cannot guarantee learning; students cannot be forced to learn; learning styles differ widely; and teachers are more important than even the most sophisticated educational tools ...' (Mellon, 1999: 34).

In the meantime, work continued in Californian garages and technology research departments on the future form of computing. By the 1960s, much of the development work that would lead to a desktop computer usable in the classroom was already complete. Although the first computers did not have monitors – they produced their output on punch tape – it had already been noted that writing could be a use for them. Rheingold (1991: 83) describes how Douglas Engelbart proposed a kind of computerised writing device in 1963. Much of the early development of word processing was completed in order to allow programmers to reconfigure hardware and write software, rather than as the creation of a tool for end-users. However, although the ideas were there, the technology to deliver it was not.

Making computers usable was a major focus for developers, and it is the success in this area that sent the PC surging into education, at least in the classrooms of enthusiasts. Engelbart, early advocate of computers for writing, also invented the mouse pointing device when working at ARC, the Augmentation Research Centre in the USA. His influence has been considerable; it would be difficult to imagine computers today without word processing or the mouse.

Drill and Practice Programs – the Early Years of Educational Software

Much of the early work on computer interfaces was influenced by psychological perspectives. The Apple Macintosh interface, in many ways the most influential graphical user interface (GUI), was produced in this way. It is largely because of the Apple Mac that we now use an icon-driven interface controlled by a mouse on all computer platforms.

Alan Kay in his work on human–computer interaction was much influenced by psychological perspectives. One of his mentors was Seymour Papert at MIT. Rheingold suggests that Kay was very much influenced by the theories of Jean Piaget, Jerome Bruner and other psychologists who were 'modelling the learning processes on the idea of exploration'.

> our minds are scientists, our senses are our instruments, the world is our experiment. The hypothesis held in common by these psychologists was that we discover the world by feeling our way around in it with all our senses, manipulating it with our hands, tracking it with our eyes and ears.
>
> (Rheingold, 1991: 85)

None of this emphasis on play, exploration and psychology seems to have transferred to the early computer programs produced for use in schools. For the most part, these were drill and practice Maths games, reading activities involving rote learning of words or spellings, interesting but aimless branching adventures and databases without content or purpose. But it was all very exciting at the time for those teachers who were open to new ways of working.

The state of school computer use in the UK during the 1980s can be better understood by examining the range of software in use in the Inner London Education Authority's schools. The ILEA had long noted that software was of critical importance in the appropriate use of computers in classrooms, and was to become a major developer of software itself. As early as 1974, the issue of educational software was being discussed in what was by then the ninth ILEA Computer Studies Newsletter:

> Computer Software Packages in Education are upon us or will be in a short while. It is of paramount importance that we understand clearly what are these packages and what are their aims. ... Where a computer software package in industry is aimed at economic efficiency and is evaluated against such an aim, a similar package in education is aimed at efficiency in learning and must be evaluated against such.

Further, the users of educational packages are generally laymen [sic] in computing matters ...

The objectives of Computer Software Packages in Education fall into one or more of the following categories.

- They allow a greater understanding of the topic under study than is possible with a conventional approach.
- They save time of learning compared with other methods to achieve the same results.
- They save teaching time.
- They allow individual learning.
- They improve teaching.
- They are cheaper.
- They provide motivation for the learner.

(Makkar, 1974: 11–12)

The writer of this summary of computer-assisted learning (CAL) indicates quite clearly what he believes to be the benefits of this way of working, and the list he offers contains some surprising suggestions in the light of later developments, particularly the assumption that CAL can be cheaper or can save teaching time. Neither of these claims is likely to be made today. The writer goes on to claim that his ideal educational software package would 'enhance learning, make no extra demand on the users and need minimal reorganisation of the existing practice' (Makkar, 1974: 13). It was to be many more years before even those far-sighted local education authorities such as ILEA recognised that the use of computers would change rather than simply support what happens in classrooms.

With the arrival of government funding for advisory teachers, this understanding of the irrevocable change capable of being brought about by computers was beginning to form part of the authority's practice. The ILEA set up the Inner London Educational Computing Centre (ILECC) and this became a national as well as regional focus for the development of educational software and classroom methodologies, especially for the RM 380Z, 480Z and Nimbus platforms of the day. At this time the main difference between LEAs was a decision to pursue either the BBC/Acorn route or the RM, later Windows PC platform. ILEA chose the latter.

By the mid-1980s, secondary schools had been given a standard network with a set of applications, and primary schools were being provided with a series of packs of software. These were usually bought by schools at a heavily subsidised price and many of the titles were little used, although others became the software equivalent of best-sellers.

By the mid-1980s the RM Nimbus computer, the successor to the 380Z and 480Z and looking not dissimilar to current PCs, was beginning to be seen in many London schools. At the same time, a decision was made to issue a pack of software at a low cost to every primary school in inner London. Considerable resources were put into providing this pack, with some of the software being specially written in London, and other titles being licensed from other LEAs or developers.

ILEA Primary Diskpack 1 was issued in summer 1986 and contained eight software titles, one or two of which still exist in some form today. Word processing had not yet developed into a one-program arena at that stage, and the wide variety of programs used is typical of those pre-Windows days. Interfaces varied widely and it could be extremely difficult to learn how to print from one program even if one knew how to do so from another.

Primary Discpack 1 – ILEA (summer 1986)
RML LOGO
Write
Idelta
Explore
L – A mathemagical adventure
Maths with a Story 1
Developing Tray
Smile 2 – The Next 17

The word processing program included in the pack, for example, was Write, which had been developed by Oxfordshire LEA. It worked on a mnemonic principle in those pre-mouse days, with key-presses of the first letter of a command being the usual method of working: P to Print, S to Save and so on. This was revolutionary in its ease of use at the time; as an Advisory Teacher at the time I well remember that printing on the 380Z had included a whole initialisation routine followed by typing 'OUTFILE LST:', hardly a memorable or intuitive command.

There was no database or spreadsheet in the first Discpack, although Idelta, a branching classification tool, was included. This had considerable potential for analysing and organising information about, for example, the environment, but its use was little understood by teachers and, unlike Write, it is not well remembered. The first version of RML LOGO was included, and it will be necessary to return to this important program below, since it is quite different in its use and in its effects than most of the other software issued in 1986. Another important program to be discussed later, ILEA Developing Tray, was also issued in this pack.

The pack was completed by a range of adventures and two Maths titles, Maths with a Story (MWAS) 1 and a set of programs called Smile 2 – The Next 17. MWAS was basically a set of numeracy games or activities, whereas Smile 2 was part of the SMILE (Secondary Maths Individualised Learning Experiment) project in London. Smile 1 and 2 had already been produced for the 480Z computer, but for some reason Smile 2 – The Next 17 was the first to appear for the RM Nimbus, which explains its rather confusing title. The Smile programs were really intended for use in secondary schools, and the fact that for some years to come some pupils would arrive in secondary schools having already used this software would remain a bone of contention between the sectors.

The adventures included in the pack were typical of the genre, a breed of program which has largely disappeared today in view of the current capabilities of moving image and sound. It is important to remember that the computers of 1986 may have looked a little like a present PC, but they displayed mostly text, they used only eight or sixteen garish colours, and pictures were infrequent and usually had jagged edges much like those seen only on Teletext systems today. The most complex adventure provided was L, which was subtitled 'A Mathemagical Adventure'. Only a minority of primary pupils found this at all accessible, but their teachers attending weekend training courses were known to sit up half the night trying to solve the mystery. Explore was rather different in that it allowed users to take part in some simple branching adventures or to devise their own.

Activity

Consider the range of titles issued to London primary schools in 1986.

- What types of software, currently considered important, are not included here?

- How do you think this range of titles would have affected teacher views of the learning potential of computers?

A year later, a second pack of software was made available to London schools. Extra copies of the pack of ten titles could be purchased for £48, a very low sum considering the number of programs involved. It is easy to forget that most costs associated with computers have fallen dramatically in real terms over the twenty years in which educational institutions have been purchasers.

Primary Discpack 2 – ILEA (summer 1987)
Quest
Grass
Ourfacts
Developing Tray
Smile – First 31

Maths with a Story 2
Puff
Martello Tower
Revolver
Adventures in the Primary Classroom
Mallory

In many ways this was a development of the first pack rather than offering very much that was new, with the exception of the inclusion of databases for the first time. Quest, developed in Hertfordshire, was a powerful database although many teachers found it difficult to use. Ourfacts and Grass were much simpler to use, but more limited in their potential. However, the inclusion of database programs in the pack enabled other advisory teachers to set up data-gathering projects such as the National Environmental Database (NED) which were to be considerably influential (Dillon, 1991; Watson and Dillon, 1995).

Also included in the second Discpack were another set of SMILE Maths programs and a second set of numeracy activities in the form of Maths with a Story (MWAS) 2. An updated version of Developing Tray was provided, as well as two new adventures: Puff, which used more pictures than had previously been the case, and Martello Tower, set in World War II and too difficult for most teachers, although not always for their students. Another kind of adventure appeared in the form of Mallory, a crime deduction program which attempted to persuade pupils to think about events within a murder scenario, rather like a computer version of the Cluedo board game. The last title, Revolver, was rather different in that it enabled schools to prepare scrolling screen displays which would look rather like the TV-based Teletext or Ceefax which were by then becoming well-known. This capability was seized on by a few schools, but the notion of using computers to publish information, albeit locally only, was an interesting development at this stage in the life of educational computing. It would be almost ten years before this activity could really take off with the arrival of the World Wide Web.

Discpacks 3 and 4 appeared almost together in autumn 1988, completing this extensive range of titles issued to all primary schools in London over a period of little more than two years. Special needs had been considered by this time, and primary school demands for a suitable spreadsheet needed to be answered.

Primary Discpack 3 – ILEA (autumn 1988)
RM LOGO 2
Paintspa
Point
Paintpot

Slide-it
Move-it
Collage
Picturecraft
Number Games
Write
Allwrite
Ted
Front Page Extra
Muddles
Compose

Primary Discpack 4 – ILEA (autumn 1988)

Key
Grasshopper
Drawmouse
Art & Time
News Bulletin
Maths Investigations
SlimWam 2
Teaching with a Micro 1–5
Random Arrivals
All Done By Numbers
Hazard and Rescue
Archipelago
Voyage to the Stars

In many ways, these two Discpacks continued the line of development set by the first two. A new version of LOGO was included, as were developments of Developing Tray in the form of All Done By Numbers and Random Arrivals. The latter two programs were part of a projected suite of variations but were never to achieve the success or penetration of the parent program; the other versions specified by the original author, Bob Moy, were never developed by the ILEA. Maths activities continued to be well represented in the form of SlimWam (Some Learning Investigations in Mathematics with a Micro) 2, Teaching with a Micro, Number Games and Maths Investigations. Databases were further developed with the addition of Key, for which large numbers of datasets had become available. In many ways, the addition of Key marked the beginning of concerns regarding access to content, concerns which would become pre-eminent ten years later as the Internet became, in effect, the database to which most pupils would turn.

For the first time, a spreadsheet was included in the pack. Grasshopper had nothing like the potential of later spreadsheets such as Excel, but its addition marked a significant moment in the development of a generic tool base at the primary stage. There were fewer adventures in these packs, although the two that were included, Archipelago and Voyage to the Stars, were produced by one of the advisory teachers working in London at the time. Hazard & Rescue provided an adventure creation program which was easy to use, adaptable and which seized the interest of many English teachers who saw its possibilities.

Word processing continued to be dominated by Oxfordshire's Write, but also included was TED, a program developed in Leicestershire LEA and including an onscreen dictionary although not yet a full-scale spell-checker. Also developed in London and included was Allwrite, the first multilingual word processing package, which allowed pupils to use computers to write in Bengali, Gujarati, Punjabi and many other languages. This program would later win an award from the British Design Council and was widely used until the constraints of the National Curriculum and other government initiatives made it ever more difficult for heritage languages to maintain their place in the classroom.

Compose was a first attempt at using the computer to create music, or in this case more correctly to assemble patterns of sound in sequences. It delighted some teachers but enraged music purists who were offended by its limitations. A further Teletext package was offered in the form of News Bulletin. The special needs programs from Birmingham LEA – Point, Slide-it, Move-it and Collage – released considerable reserves of creativity in the teachers in special and primary schools who were to devise uses for these over the next few years. Muddles provided some language activities and word games, and the packs were completed by a wide range of graphics programs. These ranged from Paintpot at the simplest end to the much more complex Drawmouse for textile and pattern design and Art & Time, which could be used for simple and very short animations. Perhaps the most widely used painting program was Paintspa, while the most complicated was Picturecraft, a combination of graphics and maths.

The four ILEA Discpacks put a wide range of software into London's schools in the mid-1980s, but it is important to recognise what they did not contain. For the most part, drill and practice software was avoided in favour of titles which were at least capable of being used in creative or expressive ways. This was extremely far-sighted, especially at a time when drill programs were very widely available. Later writing on the evaluation of software (McDougall *et al.*, 1996) has valued concentration on use rather than the attributes of a program when evaluating it, and on these grounds many of those early ILEA choices would score highly, as they would using the 'perspectives interactives paradigm' outlined in the same paper and arguing for the involvement of teachers and students with software designers. The involvement of teachers in software design is a focus for the current EC-funded PEDACTICE project (http://193.162.235.100/

pedactice/index.htm). This involvement of users had always been crucial within the ILEA and would be taken further in the case of a few programs where the ILEA was to influence the next stage in the educational use of computers.

The Exceptions – LOGO, Allwrite, Developing Tray and Collaboration

The development of LOGO by Seymour Papert has already been discussed and it is not surprising that the program formed part of the range of titles offered to London primary schools. It is Developing Tray, however, which indicates the ways in which ILEA was able to build on the expertise of its teachers. Bob Moy, teaching at Crown Woods School in south-east London, developed the ideas behind Developing Tray, and the ILEA took these up and enabled the program in its various versions to be written as a collaboration between ILECC and the English Centre in London. The result was a program which was in use by 1985 in classrooms as varied as those for infants and for sixth formers (Stephens, 1985). Reading the descriptions now of how Devtray was intended to be used, one cannot help but be struck by how things have changed in British education, now that we are increasingly being told the right way to do things. In 1985, by contrast, the devisers of Devtray were far from certain that there was one right way.

> This doesn't mean, of course, that there's one 'proper' way to run a Devtray session. Nothing in education is really like that. We've seen enough in the last four years from watching different teachers experiment with the program in their different ways to know that this could never be true. As with all powerful tools, powerful users can make quite radically different uses of it and find it serves them faithfully in all their ventures. But they do need to reflect on what is happening and to be able to 'see through' what they've started.
>
> (Moy, 1985a: 3)

Developed through action research and refined through teacher input, Devtray is a much-remembered program and indeed is still used in some classrooms today. It was designed to 'tap into some of the more central and powerful processes of language exchange that reading seemed to us to involve' (Moy, 1985a: 2). Devtray therefore came out of teacher activity and understanding of the teaching of reading, particularly based on the psycholinguistic explanations of Frank Smith (Smith, 1982) and others (Goodman, 1967), as has been explained (Moy, 1985b), rather than being the outcome of a programmer's assumption of what teaching with a computer might look like.

Allwrite, too, was an outcome of the collaborative approach taken by

LEAs such as the ILEA at this time. Teachers and students had shown the importance of making use of heritage languages in the classroom, and of the importance of bilingual texts. It was not surprising, then, that it was the ILEA who produced this innovative multilingual word-processing program, much used in the late 1980s by students, teachers, advisory services and even parents (Abbott, 1994). It was developed as a result of close collaboration between community language experts, teachers and programmers, and was to win a British Design Award – the first to be given to an educational software product – in 1991.

One of those most involved with Allwrite at the time was Diana Forster, publications manager at ILECC. She reflects here on the processes that led to its production, and its lasting achievements.

> I think the most important achievement was the raising of the status of ethnic minority languages amongst the children and adults of the ethnic minorities themselves, and in the schools where Allwrite was used. The languages offered with Allwrite were given equal billing with English and this gave people a pride in their own languages. Allwrite helped in a small way to counter the inferiority that many people from the ethnic minorities felt.

> Allwrite also gave children from the ethnic minorities a different way of expressing themselves in their own languages in the writing of stories and reports. They made signs that were displayed with their English equivalents around the school, which was one very important way in which the status of the language was raised. Printed letters were sent to ethnic minority parents in their own language which must have been a welcome development to those with a poor command of English.

> There are many reasons for a decline in the use of multilingual word-processing in schools. All the current emphasis on literacy is for literacy in English. And from some of the reports that I have heard about how word-processing is being used in schools generally, teachers have not understood its potential in helping children to write, so they will not have appreciated how creatively a program such as Allwrite could be used. (I still hear about teachers who allow children who have produced a good piece of writing to type it into the word processor and print it out as some sort of reward.) Lastly, I don't think that a Windows version of Allwrite was ever produced, and using a DOS program on a Windows machine these days will be beyond the capabilities of most primary school teachers, if it is possible at all.
>
> (Diana Forster, e-mail to the author, 1 March 2000)

Teacher collaboration in the production of software was a key facet of the ILEA's work, and of many other British LEAs at the time. By the mid-1990s, however, software production was increasingly in other hands. Diana Forster is now working in a senior position in multimedia publishing; like most of those who once worked within IT support in a local education authority, she is now employed in the commercial sector. LEAs do not, for the most part, operate as significant resource developers in the current UK market.

Drill and Practice Returns – the ILS Phenomenon

Towards the end of the term of office of the last Conservative government, a delegation visited the USA to consider the uses of computers in schools there. A number of issues were noted in the report of that visit (NCET, 1993), and some of these issues were further developed in two following publications (NCET, 1994a, 1994b). Following the US visit, an evaluation programme was set up to consider the potential of Integrated Learning Systems (ILSs) in the UK context.

It was decided that two main products would be involved in the evaluation: a well-established American ILS called Success Maker and a much more recent British product, Global Learning. The evaluation eventually lasted for three years and other products were considered in the later stages. The ILS evaluation is important as much for the fact that it happened as for what it may or may not have shown about the products concerned. No UK government had previously arranged such an evaluation of an educational software product, and the initial stages of the process were marked by considerable concern amongst the UK educational software publishers. Their concerns were linked to the decline in US school software purchases at the end of the 1980s when ILS was at its zenith there.

ILS began in the USA in the 1970s and the term can cover a wide variety of products and systems. In most cases, an ILS is characterised by a wide variety of content in the form of exercises and activities, linked to a complex management system which tracks and records learner activity, success, perseverance and time spent on the system. By its very nature, an ILS has to be an individual learning activity, and it thus runs counter to the more European tradition of collaborative and provisional use of computers. The classic ILS is much more concerned with certainties and correct answers than it is with provisionalities and discursive learning.

In most cases, ILSs are targeted at those for whom literacy and numeracy have become a problem. They are seen as remediation tools rather than initial learning experiences, and the content they offer is in most cases a rather more sophisticated and graphically diverse version of the drill and practice activities of the 1970s. This is hardly surprising given the necessity for learner responses to be capable of automatic correction; computers allow little room for uncertainties and provisional drafts. Most of the systems developed in the USA work on an essentially behaviourist model, with an assumption that a high success rate of 75 per cent correct or better is needed in order to maintain interest and motivation. If the success rate falls below this pre-set level, then more accessible tasks are presented. This may be appropriate in a US context but seems less so in the European one, where collaboration may be more sought after than competition. In any case, the success rate of particular systems is kept confidential by the developers, making it difficult for teachers to come to an effective decision about applicability for their own students.

In the majority of ILS-using schools it is assumed that learners will access the system for a set period each day, usually of around forty minutes. If all learners in a year group, or more usually all learners assessed as below a particular standardised level, are to do so, then a finite number of multimedia computers will be required. These computers must be equipped with sound cards, CDROM drives and headphones, and will need to be upgraded regularly. Investing in ILS is a hardware as well as a software decision, and it is hardly surprising that the British distributor for Success Maker is RM, the most successful supplier of hardware to the UK educational system.

The claims made by the producers of Integrated Learning Systems – renamed by some developers as Individualised Learning Systems – are considerable. The US advertising tends to have a greater air of certainty than advertising elsewhere, although this may be a reflection of different legal frameworks regarding such publicity.

Success Maker was developed by the Computer Curriculum Corporation (CCC), who are a major multimedia publisher. In the way of publishing companies in the last few years, they are in turn owned by a series of interlocking multinational publishing companies who in fact also own some of the competing ILS products. Success Maker is advertised in the USA as being a foundation in 'the basics'. The advertising literature refers to the acquisition of key concepts, problem-solving strategies and continuous progress assessment. More recently, a course within Success Maker called Choosing Success has been targeted particularly at students at risk. This student group is not defined in the literature, but most of the illustrations are of ethnic minority group members.

> The numbers are staggering and the problem is growing. More than three million students are at risk of dropping out of school, with devastating consequences to themselves and society alike. Confronted with personal or societal conflicts, most of these students want to succeed in school – and in life – but sometimes they just don't have the skills to do so.
>
> (*Choosing Success*, CCC advertising brochure, 1994)

This is educational software as rather more than computer-assisted learning; the model here is of the system as an agent for social re-engineering. It is a claim which will engender considerable scepticism, at least in some national markets. At around the same time (1994) Success Maker was being advertised in the US educational computing press with the slogan 'Imagine if our kids' test scores were as high as their Nintendo scores'. The small print in the advertisement refuted claims that Success Maker is about 'drilling and killing' and went on to describe the system as 'educational insurance', a powerful model to sell to educational administrators, especially in a litigious society such as the USA. The advertisement ends on an upbeat note which seems to take the reader far away from the reality of the repetitive and uninteresting activities which many have found in ILS.

> So we will do more than promise your students will achieve the results in the predicted time. We guarantee it. ... Kids already have the technology to challenge their reflexes. Isn't it about time they had the technology to challenge their minds? EXPECT GREAT THINGS.
> (Advertisement in *The Computing Teacher*, USA, 1994)

Some research has been quite positive about the use of ILS (Fischer, 1996), but in this case the course described was a specialised one taken at university level. The course was set up with considerable grant funding from the manufacturers, a process which has occurred in other ILS projects and research. Fischer also makes many assumptions that may not be fully justified by the research, including the assertion that 'ILS will clearly pay a major role in the classrooms of the twenty-first century' (Fischer, 1996: 71).

Success Maker is distributed internationally in Canada, New Zealand and Australia, as well as in the UK. The advertising in the UK is very different from that in Success Maker's home country. As in the US advertising, quotations from teachers were included. The tone was very different, however, even though the product being sold was exactly the same.

> Success Maker is built on a 25-year research and development in the classroom [sic]. It provides a private environment, individualised courses and a system of constant feedback on progress and rewards for success. ...

> Its twenty-five year development programme has given Success Maker unparalleled diagnostic and instructional routines providing individualised courses of study for each student. The outcomes of Success Maker are real learning gains for the individual with sophisticated tracking of student progress and forecasting of future development.
> (RM promotional leaflet, 1994)

The UK pilot evaluation of ILS was managed by the National Council for Educational Technology and took place from January to July 1994. The report of that evaluation contains a useful definition of an ILS.

> An integrated learning system (ILS) is a computer-based system that manages the delivery of curriculum material to students so that they are presented with individual programmes of work. The materials are often computer-based, but not exclusively so. The system provides feedback to students as they work and detailed records for both students and tutor. Systems contain diagnostic elements that facilitate individual learning programmes. They usually have an on-line management system that enables a number of students to work on the system at the same time, at different levels, to receive immediate feedback on progress and, when needed, provide students with appropriate tutorial and practice sessions.
>
> (Detheridge, 1994: 9)

The first year's evaluation, adopting a familiar researcher strategy, indicated the inconclusiveness of its findings and the need for further research. The evaluation eventually ran for three years, although different products were considered by various teams of researchers and the whole process has itself been the subject of further research (Wood *et al.*, 1999). Throughout the process, the aim was to evaluate ILS generally, not individual products, but it proved very difficult to separate these two things.

The final report of the evaluation was written by a researcher from one university and drew upon the work of colleagues from the nine UK institutions which had by then been involved. The report begins with a statement from BECTa (British Educational Communications and Technology Agency, the successor to NCET), indicating caution as a suitable approach to ILS. This was in marked contrast to the upbeat pronouncements made, particularly by politicians, at the beginning of the evaluation. By 1998, however, both the government and the targets for ICT had changed, and the new Labour government had other agendas for computer use. The conclusions of the final evaluation are measured and cautious.

- There is considerable evidence that pupils do learn from integrated learning systems. The main issue is not if pupils learn but what and how they learn.
- The use of ILS has a marked and positive effect on pupils' attitudes, motivation and behaviour. As yet evidence is inconclusive as to whether these positive impacts generalise beyond experience with

ILS to influence more general attitudes towards schooling or school subjects.

- Where the use of ILS at least matches what can be achieved with conventional teaching, it offers a stimulating means of extending the range of learning opportunities open to pupils. However, the results suggest that exclusive reliance on ILS for preparation for Key Stage Three tests and GCSE exams may have a negative impact, and imply that non-ILS teaching is pedagogically necessary during the period of immediate preparation for these examinations.

- Although teachers and headteachers were generally positive in their attitudes towards ILS and its educational impact, there are issues to address concerning the apparent gap between the acquisition and evaluation of core skills and the wider knowledge and skills tested in the examination performance.

- There was evidence from all three phases of evaluation that ILS can help to enhance teachers' confidence in IT and contribute to the development of their knowledge and skills in the management and use of educational technology.

(Wood, 1998: 7)

A paper by Wood *et al.* (1999) further examines the evaluation process from the perspective of those researchers who were involved in it. This overview and critique of the UK ILS evaluation suggests that the conclusions above obscure very different findings in each year. The paper argues for a new understanding of the need for appropriate research contexts in this area, rather than a situation where 'variability should, seemingly, be the norm' (Wood *et al.*, 1999: 95). The slight and arguable evidence of learning achievement from ILS nevertheless attracted a great deal of attention from policy makers and politicians. One cannot help but compare this with the slow progress towards individual ownership of computers, despite the clear evidence (Phillips *et al.*, 1999; Robertson *et al.*, 1997) of the value of palmtops for pupils or notebook computers for teachers.

Activity

Consider the definition of an ILS given in this first UK evaluation document. ILS went on to attract a considerable amount of interest. The popular press and politicians were very much attracted to it. Why do you think this might be? More surprisingly to some observers, most of the teachers in schools that piloted ILS in the UK also became firm advocates of it. How would you explain this?

ICT as Tool or Teaching Machine

The argument about the comparative values of the teaching of IT as a discrete subject or its use across the curriculum is a long-lasting discussion which shows no sign of coming to resolution. It is linked to the similarly unresolved issue of computer labs or computers in classrooms (Watson, 1990). Bill Gates is certainly not an advocate of the former, describing computer labs as an arrangement leading to little PC use, and arguing instead for a rapid move to integrating the PC throughout the curriculum (Gates 1999: 388) – with all of those PCs presumably running Microsoft Windows.

It is interesting to note that Gates chooses to feature a school from the UK to demonstrate his ideas, for it is the UK that has been the leader among those nations seeking to use ICT across the curriculum. He writes too of Israel and Costa Rica, but he could also have mentioned Denmark or Hungary, but innovation in those countries is much less often celebrated than innovation in the G7 nations and other groupings, due to their comparative anonymity on the world scene.

Individual access – a computer for every student – started (Gates 1999) in Australia at the beginning of the 1990s when one school in Melbourne was extremely influential. Later state-wide projects in areas such as Victoria kept the influence of Australia strong in this area of development.

Activity

Ten hard lessons on computers in schools

1   Computer labs are a lousy place for computers. They need to be in classrooms.
2   Struggling students often get more out of computers than higher performers.
3   Most teachers still haven't been trained on how to use computers in class.
4   School systems must plan computer use carefully.
5   Computers are a tool, not a subject. They need to be integrated into the lessons of other subjects.
6   Kids flourish when everyone has a computer.
7   Hand-me-down machines are not good enough for school use.
8   Computers don't diminish traditional skills.
9   The Internet and e-mail excite kids by giving them an audience.
10 Kids love computers.
          (*Wall Street Journal*, November 1997, quoted in Gates 1999: 402)

This was written to describe the situation in the USA. Does it also hold good in your own experience of education? With which of these statements do you agree?

Gates remarks too, as have so many observers, on the notable lack of damage sustained by personally owned laptops, although he does report the bizarre phenomenon of screens damaged when pens are trapped inside folding laptops. One wonders for what the students needed the pens when using their computers.

Training companies whose task is to pass on information and procedures rather than to educate have often been quicker to embrace technology than have more traditional educational institutions. As has often been pointed out, there are some aspects of training that online delivery can support both efficiently and effectively:

> An online catalog of courses and an online registration system take the pain out of class registration. People can view course descriptions and the dates and times the courses are offered; find out whether a class is full and how long the waiting list is; and ask to be notified by e-mail when particular classes they're interested in will be offered. When people register online, they can add a class to their electronic schedules with the click of a button. When the course is over, each participant can be sent an electronic survey to evaluate the course's effectiveness. Freed of managing most of the logistics, trainers and administrators can concentrate on course content.
>
> (Gates 1999: 249)

But how much of this can be modelled within the school environment? It would be the Internet that began to offer some possible answers to that question by the late 1990s, and it is to the Internet and the hype which sometimes surrounds the use of computers that we will turn in the next chapter.

Chapter Summary

- Most educational systems respond slowly and with some scepticism to new technologies.
- Much of the early use of computers in school was based on behaviourist thinking and involved for the most part drill and practice programs.
- In the UK, the local education authorities were crucial in supporting and guiding the use of computers in classrooms, especially in the years before local management of schools diluted their influence.
- Programs such as LOGO and Developing Tray, the exceptions among a sea of drill activities, have tended to survive while less powerful programs have not.

- Integrated Learning Systems have attracted a great deal of interest, but this attention is related to political aims and popular notions of literacy and numeracy, rather than to ideas about the effective use of ICT.
- As ICT has become more pervasive in all aspects of Western society, business leaders have begun to seek to influence educational systems.

Bibliography

Abbott, C. (1994). *Look, that's my Language: Word-processing for a Multilingual Society*. Paper presented at NECC '94, Boston, USA.

Detheridge, T. (ed.) (1994). *Integrated Learning Systems: A Report of the Pilot Evaluation of ILS in the UK*. Coventry: NCET.

Dillon, J. (1991) The National Environmental Database Project. *Computer Education*, 67, 3–4.

Fischer, M. J. (1996). ILS: an application linking technology with human factors and pedagogical principles. *Educational Technology Research and Development*, 44 (3), 65–72.

Gates, B. (1999). *Business Using a Digital Nervous System*. London: Penguin.

Goodman, K. (1967). Reading: a psycholinguistic guessing game. *Journal of the Reading Specialist*, 4, 126–35.

McDougall, A., Squires, D. and Guss, S. (1996). Emphasising use over attributes in the selection of educational software. *Education and Information Technologies*, 1, 151–64.

Makkar, L. (1974). Education and computer software packages. *ILEA Computer Studies Newsletter*, 9, 11–13.

Mellon, C. A. (1999). Technology and the great pendulum of education. *Journal of Research on Computing in Education*, 32 (1), 28–35.

Moy, B. (1985a). Introduction. In J. Stephens (ed.), *Devtray Teaching Documents* (2–3). London: ILEA.

—— (1985b). Thinking under the influence. In J. Stephens (ed.), *Devtray Teaching Documents* (4–5). London: ILEA.

—— (1993). *Seen IT in the USA*. Coventry: NCET.

—— (1994a). *Seen IT in Australia*. Coventry: NCET.

—— (1994b). *Seen IT in the UK*. Coventry: NCET.

Phillips, R., Bailey, M., Fisher, T. and Harrison, C. (1999). Questioning teachers about their use of portable computers. *Journal of Computer Assisted Learning*, 15, 149–61.

Rheingold, H. (1991). *Virtual Reality*. London: Secker & Warburg.

Robertson, S., Calder, J., Fung, P., Jones, A. and O'Shea, T. (1997). The use and effectiveness of palmtop computers in education. *British Journal of Educational Technology*, 28(3), 177–89.

Smith, F. (1982). *Writing and the Writer*. New York: Holt, Rinehart & Winston.

Stephens, J. (ed.) (1985). *Devtray Teaching Documents*. London: ILEA.

Watson, D. M. (1990). The classroom vs. the computer room. *Computers and Education*, 15 (1), 33–7.

Watson, R. and Dillon, J. (eds.) (1995). *National Environmental Database Project*. Harwell: Atomic Energy Authority.

Wood, D. (1998). *The UK ILS Evaluations: Final Report.* Coventry: BECTa.
Wood, D., Underwood, J. and Avis, P. (1999). Integrated learning systems in the classroom. *Computers and Education*, 33, 91–108.

6 The Rise of the Internet and the Race to Connect

The Hype and the Reality

If the use of computers in education has often been bedevilled by alternating between wild claims and dismissive remarks, then the more recent development of the use of those computers to access the Internet has seen this alternation of extremes become ever more exaggerated. The proponents and opponents of Internet use in schools, aptly described in one recent book as the 'cybercritics' and the 'cybertopians' (Papert, 1996), have consumed large areas of media coverage in newspapers and on television. Generalised criticisms of the claimed potential of the Internet to transform society (Stoll, 1995) have been followed by more measured and specific critical analysis of current policy (Selwyn, 1998).

Selwyn has also suggested that researchers into the use of computers in education in general have too often been seen as enthusiasts for and advocates of ICT rather than truly impartial: 'IT (along with technology in general) has been unique in educational terms inasmuch as, unlike any other innovation, its benefit to schools and colleges has remained largely unchallenged' (Selwyn, 1998: 424).

Selwyn is certainly doing his best to change this, having published a version of his concerns in more than one journal, and it is undoubtedly true that although there has been substantive research in this area (Cox, 1993; Watson, 1993), it has been quantitative for the most part, and much else has been insubstantial and unsubstantiated. The publication of a large-scale research project in the USA, Teaching and Learning with Computers, led by Henry Becker, is likely to be of interest and should add considerably to the evidence base in this area (http://www.crito.uci.edu/tlc/html/tlc_home.html).

What has been described as the 'overly optimistic tone' (Selwyn, 1997: 305) of much educational computing research is linked with the claims often made for the Internet. Selwyn (1997) also argues against the historic emphasis on quantitative and case study research in this area at the expense of ethnographic and qualitative approaches. He claims to perceive a 'distrust and avoidance of theory' (Selwyn, 1997: 306). More recently, and writing with a colleague (Gorard and Selwyn, 1999), he has considered the wider context of the learning society and moves towards lifelong learning. Gorard and Selwyn locate the proposed University for Industry within the hype surrounding ICT and society's belief in it. They claim that 'societal belief in IT as a technical fix has blighted the successful integration of ICT into the educational system over the last twenty years' (Gorard and Selwyn, 1999: 531).

The Rise of the Internet

Much of the early discussion of the Internet related to its effect on modes of writing and the extent to which it might change the way in which society relates to texts. This relationship with texts is a central concern of schooling, but it was to be several years before the Internet debate moved on to become centred around schools, children and online learning. Much journalism and some academic writing about the Internet has fallen into one of two categories: illusory hype, sometimes aptly termed 'cyberbole', or pessimistic Armageddon. The computer, we are told 'has allowed the bourgeoisie to fall in love once again with the future' (Boal, 1995: 7). On the other hand, there is a reputable basis for some of the pessimism, and we are reminded (Heim, 1993: 55) that it was Heidegger who described the twentieth century as being intimately concerned with the confrontation between global technology and European humanity, although he was suggesting this before the appearance of much current technology and liberal humanist views of it.

Discussing the differing views of the hype and the 'jeremiads', Drew suggests that much of the debate is centred around privileged forms of behaviour:

> The mass media usually limit the critical response to this celebration of new communication technology to academics who accuse the new electronic media of eroding a past, higher civilisation of print-based culture. Much of the writing of this group calls for curtailing the new technologies. In an earlier time, their counterparts lamented the rise of the paperback book and its 'cheapening of culture'.
>
> (Drew, 1995: 75)

Occasionally, however, thoughtful pieces of writing have appeared in a number of publications, most particularly in the mid-1990s as use of the World Wide Web began to be widespread, and as journalists began to gain access to it. Examination of some articles from this period gives a flavour of the discourse as it developed.

The early 1990s tended to be a defensive time and the focus was on the effect that ICT and the Internet might have on books, periodicals and libraries. Journalists were quick to cover stories of impending doom for the book, perhaps aware that their own lives and livelihoods might be threatened. Their reaction to electronic writing might seem surprising until we realise that at this time many of them did not have access to such tools themselves, at least in the early years of the decade. Even William Gibson's seminal electronic text *Agrippa (Book of the Dead)*, a text firmly based within traditional literary practices but delivered electronically, was described as 'self-destructive' (Dannatt, 1992) in an article in the arts pages of *The Independent* newspaper, in which Dannatt profiled Gibson, coiner of the term 'cyberspace'.

Metaphors such as cyberspace are powerful agents for the setting of scene and the creation of an aura around a particular activity. Other writers have drawn attention to the consistent use of the metaphor of a conduit when talking about language (Reddy, 1979; Street, 1988) and the linked metaphor, an essentially geographical one, of cyberspace as some kind of place is a persuasive, pervading and persisting one. Miller (1995) reminds us of the human propensity to form geographical entities in order to understand consciousness. The metaphor which interests her most, however, is the rather more gendered term 'frontier'. Unlike cyberspace, a new coinage which carries only a faint aura of science fiction, the word 'frontier' brings with it connotations of something which we should strive to pass or go beyond – or at least that some of us should. A frontier is, says Miller, 'on the verge of being acquired; currently unowned, but still ownable. Just as the ideal of chastity makes virginity sexually provocative, so does the unclaimed territory invite settlers, irresistibly so' (Miller, 1995: 51).

Miller goes on to make the fascinating point that a further similarity between geographical and digital frontiers is that, for each to be settled and made safe, women and children apparently have to be protected. In a passage written before writers such as Dale Spender had begun to challenge the image of the helpless online female, Miller writes perceptively: 'If on-line women successfully contest these attempts to depict them as the beleaguered prey of brutish men, expect the pedophile to assume a large profile in arguments that the Net is out of control' (Miller, 1995: 52).

More importantly, since Gibson was widely covered in the newspapers at the time, Dannatt adds to his article an extra and separate section which looks to the future and the advent of what he supposes will be virtual libraries. Dannatt and others (Abbott, 1994) were sometimes criticised as futurologists at the time when they suggested this, but much of what they predicted has now taken place, with the arrival of electronic libraries and digital portable books, the latter having appeared in the USA and Japan in 1999 and in Europe in 2000. The UK government, after all, has a policy of Internet connection for all libraries by 2002, and has made £50,000,000 available for the digitisation of content.

Dannatt's article describes the development of Gibson's oeuvre, its characterisation by the term 'cyberpunk', and its rapid acquisition of large numbers of fervent and devoted fans. He explains the publishing methodology planned for *Agrippa (Book of the Dead)*, only available on disk, and its extra frisson for the reader when it erased itself as it was read. A collaboration between Gibson and an artist, Dennis Ashbaugh, *Agrippa* was extremely influential. It was important both for its effect on the artistic community, who began to see the potential of electronic media, and for the extent to which it entered public consciousness.

Dannatt was one of the first journalists to highlight the potential for change that electronic communications can bring to other media. By doing so he seemed to be avoiding two traps, impending doom or glorious metamorphosis, into which so many of his colleagues had staggered. Dannatt explores the phenomenon of what he terms 'floppy-back' publishing, whereby writers who would not otherwise be published can make their work available on disk; and he notes that the first book published in this way was a memoir by a Vietnam war veteran. This volume later appeared in hardback. When dealing with the economics of disk publishing, Dannatt highlights the paradoxical situation of costs being low for the publisher, but the reader having publishing options too.

Unlike most writers who covered *Agrippa* in 1992, he also discusses the content of the story, and in doing so raises some points which were not noticed by others:

> whatever the technology behind such 'hypertexts' it still comes down to the quality of the writing. In fact Gibson has rescued the project from being a flashy gimmick by the metaphorical connection his story makes between its process and content. Agrippa is a short memoir of his father, a man who died when Gibson was a child, and is based around an old photo album he discovered on a visit to his West Virginia home (Agrippa was one of several historic trademark names used by Kodak in the twenties).
>
> (Dannatt, 1992)

The metaphorical connection that Gibson develops is that the act of reading the disk is an act of transfer, with what is at first only a digital memory on a computer disk then becoming a human memory contained in a reader's mind, a system, says Dannatt, with 'a less efficient, but more mysterious retrieval technique'.

Further paradoxes and contradictions arise, as Dannatt points out, from the inability of such a project to fit in with the requirements of libraries and archives; what library would wish to store a book which would be destroyed the first time it was read? It is Dannatt's realisation of the effect of such technological possibilities on the libraries of the future that makes this article such a far-sighted one for the date at which it appeared. The arrival of the World Wide Web, only one year after this article was written, laid the ground for a rapid rise in self-publishing to an extent never before possible; electronic communications and not electronic storage became the key to publishing in this media. Dannatt comes close to foreseeing this towards the end of his article:

> Yet the most promising development for the future has been the hardest to foretell. This is the rise of electronic mail exchanges as a means of collective self-expression. They are more spontaneous than normal writing, more considered than speech. Anyone who has worked in an office knows how irresistible is digital flirtation.
>
> (Dannatt, 1992)

The Internet and Textual Devices

During the mid-1990s many articles were published examining the particular characteristics of writing on the Internet and its reliance on devised icons to express emotion (Fielding, 1994; Sutcliffe, 1993). Sutcliffe's main subject in his Glossary column, dealing with what he described as changes in language, was shared with many articles in late 1993 and in 1994: the small pictures constructed from punctuation marks and intended to convey added meaning to electronic texts. Later to be known as emoticons, they are described as smileys by Sutcliffe. He sees these symbols as a benign development, generated, he says, 'by the need to add human character to the lifeless characters on the computer screen'. This is a theory shared by many other observers, although not the only explanation for the appearance of emoticons. They can be seen as the equivalent of schoolboy pig Latin or backslang, textual gateway devices designed to keep out newcomers and solidify the membership qualities of current users. Sutcliffe also notes in this article a central problem for all users of electronic messaging systems:

> One of the interesting things about electronic mail is how difficult it is to have any control over how it is received. You may wing off a sprightly, teasing reference to some recent event and what you get back is a wounded notice to quit, furious at your bullying tone. Emoticons are designed to prevent such misunderstandings.
>
> (Sutcliffe, 1993)

Sutcliffe adopts the term 'baudy language' to describe the whole area of emoticons and associated usages. He suggests that human language is adopting metaphors from computer use and vice versa, at least where all participants in the discourse have the necessary pre-knowledge to understand the analogy. He quotes examples in use at companies such as Apple and Microsoft, and goes on to surmise that not only are computers becoming more human but that human beings are becoming more like computers.

As Sutcliffe realises, this area of discussion includes much that is relevant to work in the area of Artificial Intelligence (AI). Since the development of the very early computer program Eliza, which attempted to produce a simulacrum of human speech, one aspect of AI which has attracted a great deal of interest is that of the production of human-like dialogue. It was to be the late 1990s before products which relied on speech input were available to education sites.

Discussion of emoticons should also recognise the links between this area and that of body language, also a series of support signs but used to support spoken rather than written language. Emoticons can be seen as a humanising factor, mediating between writer and reader, and attempting to bring both together. There are complex issues here of politeness and what has been described as 'face' (Brown and Levinson, 1987), and emoticons have been seen by many writers as key indicators of online practice. Others, especially Kress, have drawn attention to the changes in communication which have led to the visual becoming more important within the range of communicative texts (Kress and Leeuwen, 1996).

Some writers at this time were beginning to look at digital communication practices in context and were also looking at the effect they were having on non-digital processes. Helen Fielding developed some of these ideas and added some of her own in an article dealing with the social codes of the computerised workplace (Fielding, 1994). Adopting the term 'Netiquette', soon to be scattered over a hundred similar articles, Fielding emphasised the human effect of the kinds of communication being mediated. After explaining the exponential growth of users and the danger of being misinterpreted, Fielding discussed the phenomenon of flaming, those angry discourses which can simmer for months and are often triggered by a simple misunderstanding of meaning, tone or ironic interpolation.

Fielding also quotes George McMurdo (Queen Margaret College, Edinburgh) who has researched the effects of e-mail. McMurdo is reported by Fielding as having noted the way in which e-mail is seen as being positive by most companies, improving communication, making people more approachable and saving time and money. Interestingly, by the late 1990s the mood had changed, with many large corporations putting curbs on personal e-mail use and attempting to limit e-mail discussions to the strictly professional arena. Fielding talked to a number of consultants and observers about the ways in which new moralities are applied to electronic communication, with confidentiality being routinely breached and informality the rule rather than the exception. She found new patterns of conduct which related to the informality of e-mail and the brevity of most messages, together creating what she believes to be a powerful mode of communication.

Interestingly, Fielding also mentions emoticons but sees them as the devices of a subculture, badges for club members, rather than as an aid to communication. She notes the existence of another group for whom emoticons are 'a sign of lazy and inadequate use of language'. It is interesting to see a female writer making this point, for most of the proponents of emoticons are male, many of them the adult versions of the same schoolboys who whiled away the journey to school by discoursing in backslang or special words known only to themselves and their coterie. Perhaps emoticons, rather than being an aid to communication and understanding, simply developed in order to allow men to continue to communicate in the ways in which they have always done?

For Jay David Bolter, an authority on the development of the relationship of writing and the computer (Bolter, 1991), emoticons are iconic faces and they play the role of providing context for verbal text and of avoiding misunderstanding. The writer, he suggests, 'tries to enforce a univocal interpretation on prose that is otherwise open to many interpretations' (Bolter, 1996: 108). He goes on to argue that the model for this kind of writing is therefore conversation, perhaps in its telephonic form, rather than writing. He supports this assertion by reminding his readers that written forms have never seemed to need to develop such iconic assistance except in a few texts such as Laurence Sterne's *Tristram Shandy*, in which blank pages and typesetting irregularities are used for effect or, to a lesser extent, in Lewis Carroll's *Alice's Adventures in Wonderland*, in which the poem about the mouse is presented in the shape of the mouse's tail. One might also add the concrete poetry which was a popular form in the 1960s, and the wheel could be said to have come full circle with the use by current popular novelists of changes of typeface to indicate e-mail conversations or online chat (Coupland, 1995). By 1999, it was even possible for a major Hollywood studio to release a feature film called *You've Got Mail*, secure in the knowledge that a large proportion of the potential audience would recognise the reference as being to a popular e-mail program.

Bolter proposes that the use of emoticons 'suggests that contemporary electronic writers are not interested in the distancing and ambiguity that prose offers' (Bolter, 1996: 108). While this may well be accurate, a counter-assertion could be made that these writers may be interested in other ambiguities and distancing practices which this medium alone can provide: ambiguities of gender, for example, and the adoption of multiple personalities and identities, a practice which is extremely attractive to young people who may enjoy the opportunity to try out different selves online.

Activity

- To what extent does it seem to you that the young people you teach are experimenting with different identities at various times and places?
- Do parents recognise in the reports you write the same son or daughter they know at home?
- What might be the positive and negative outcomes of a place such as the Internet where possibilities for assuming multiple identities are considerable?

The Race to Connect – National Policies

Countries around the world have raced to connect their schools and classrooms to the Internet. Bill Gates describes connected learning communities as central to his vision of a digital nervous system, and quotes approvingly the words of Reed Hundt, Chairman of the US Federal Communications Commission: 'Our national commitment to connect every classroom in every school in the country to the Internet will be the greatest advance in quality and equality of education in this country' (Gates, 1999: 387).

At the same time as online learning has seemed to minimise the importance of geography, at least in the developed world, governments have also begun to re-examine concepts of education and learning. Increasingly, universities have developed modular courses to encourage accrual of qualifications by incremental steps, and governments have developed this idea further by notions such as the UK's proposed University for Industry. Promises of lifelong learning have entered the policy documents of many nations, as have indications that the Internet, in one form or another, is important to all groups in society.

Concerns have grown about the position of what have become known as the information haves and have-nots. It has been suggested (Bier *et al.*, 1997) that low-income families in Florida, given Internet access as part of a research project, showed 'powerful transformations' and gained 'empowerment' in ways not fully specified. Other writing, related to the concerns about who does and does not have access (Becker and Ravitz, 1998), has shown that within any grouping, whatever the social background, the high-ability pupils will dominate in terms of Internet access. Becker goes on to note that it is difficult to research this area since the Internet is as yet an example of an 'immature technologically-imbedded [sic] innovation' (Becker and Ravitz, 1998: 4) of a kind which inevitably produces inequalities.

Around the world, educational systems are attempting to respond to what they all recognise as a major development. In the UK, the National Grid for Learning (NGfL) has sought to represent a bridgehead for state education in this area, but by 1998 it had to be relaunched as a result of revised thinking about its aims and objectives. By 2000 a further change was signalled with the intention of making the Grid into a contributory database to which teachers would submit resources, rather as had been the approach when the equivalent to the Grid, ScoilNet (http://www.scoilnet.ie/), was launched in Ireland.

In 1998, the UK government began a major programme of installing fast Internet access (ISDN2 or better) in all schools, and insisting on and funding ICT training for all current and future teachers. The programme, costing in excess of one billion pounds and funded by the Department for Education and Employment and the Department of Culture, Media and Sport, the latter through the National Lottery Opportunities Fund, dwarfed anything that had gone before. It was matched by similar initiatives in many other countries.

In its proposals published under the title *Connecting the Learning Society* (DfEE, 1997) the UK government, through the Department for Education and Employment, set out a series of targets which would be the aims for the five-year period leading up to 2002, shortly before the next general election. These related for the most part to education, but some of the targets also took account of an apparent concern to involve the whole age range of society in life-long learning with technology. The targets can be summarised as follows:

- A National Grid for Learning, to be at least partially implemented by 1998.
- All newly-qualified teachers ICT-literate by 1999.
- All serving teachers confident and competent with ICT by 2002.
- Schools, colleges, universities, libraries and many community centres connected to the NGfL by 2002. Also at least 75 per cent of teachers and 50 per cent of students to have their own e-mail addresses.
- Most school leavers to have a good understanding of ICT by 2002.
- By 2002 the UK to be a centre of excellence for networked software content for education and lifelong learning.
- All communications between institutions and government to be electronic by 2002

(Summarised from DfEE, 1997: 24–5)

In order to implement these targets, schools were also required to submit ICT development plans, as were Local Education Authorities (LEAs). A requirement was placed on the DfEE to collect accurate statistical information about progress, and to avoid, for example, including outdated hardware in this data. The relevant curriculum and assessment agencies were asked to reassess the role of ICT in the areas for which they were responsible, museums and galleries were asked to consider their input to the Grid, and a continuing programme of evaluation of the scheme was promised. At the same time, writers such as Sefton-Green began to call for a re-examination of digital arts in the curriculum and a more secure role for the humanities and ICT (Sefton-Green, 1999).

Activity – the Seven NGfL Targets

- How many of the targets have been achieved in your school?
- Which are likely to be the most difficult to achieve?
- Consider any changes in your school related to new technologies which are not indicated in these targets.
- What might a post-2002 target list look like?

Before considering the appropriateness of this series of actions in view of the online activities described in this study, it is necessary to summarise progress made by 2000. Most plans appeared to be on target, with considerable amounts of new equipment having been installed in schools over the first two years in which money was available for this from the DfEE Standards Fund. All teacher education institutions had been told to give Qualified Teacher Status only to those students who demonstrated the appropriate level of ICT capability. The ambitious plan to use funds from the National Lottery (the New Opportunities Fund) for training all teachers was looking more likely to be flawed however, with a serious shortfall in the number of providers involved. The catalogue of providers issued to schools in April 1999 listed 158 training providers rather than the 200 predicted by the Teacher Training Agency (TTA), and many of these planned to offer training only in some parts of the country. No trainers bid to be involved in training teachers on the use of ICT with children with severe or complex learning needs, and a second round of tendering took place in 1999 before this area could be adequately covered.

The promised CDROM for Teacher Needs Identification failed to appear from the TTA within the time-scale promised, amidst much rumour and conjecture about waste of funding and the need to start again. When it did appear, the reaction was mixed, although many of those charged with supporting teachers recognised the value it gave in providing good-quality video evidence to use on training courses. It seems likely that the very short time-scale for all the Grid targets listed was beginning to affect the quality of outcomes. By mid-1999, there were already signs of tension in the leadership of this whole area, which had involved considerable investment.

A cursory summary of the above would be that these were ambitious plans partially implemented but with serious flaws; the kind of situation which OFSTED might describe as adequate but with considerable room for improvement. The programme to train all teachers seems central to any examination of these plans. If young people in future are to be more persuaded than were previous generations that the education system understands and can make good use of online communication and information, then this can only be achieved by appropriate teacher education. Teachers need to be helped to see the possibilities, and encouraged to explore the potential for themselves; just as the young people they teach have been exploring that potential for some years. What will not have the required effect is a programme of entirely skills-based rather than reflective teacher education, and choice of training provider will be extremely relevant to the effectiveness of this area. It might also be appropriate for those young people who are the experts here to themselves become the teachers in the process.

An examination of the government targets in the light of how young people use ICT may prove helpful in assessing the likely effectiveness of what is proposed. If the proposals do not take account of the modes of operation and practices which are part of everyday online life for many young people, then these targets are likely to prove inadequate.

These online practices are part of everyday life for the young people who currently inhabit the online world which the government seeks to make a site of formal state education. Change, a constant state of flux, is not a passing phase but the natural environment online. Young digerati expect to change everything frequently, to discard what has been shown to be less than effective, or to begin anew simply to try something different. The archetypal government academic model of piloting something, evaluating it and only then implementing it, is hardly likely to be embraced by such young people. In their world, implementation often comes first, evaluation is informal, though often extensive in the form of guestbooks and other direct communication with users, and may lead to summary abandonment, and piloting hardly exists at all, unless in the form of Web sites labelled as 'under construction'.

It is a natural propensity of governments to seek to enshrine good practice and preserve it by resisting change; governments are much more concerned with conservation than they are with changing things. It is not only that words such as 'revolution' have been applied to what is happening to information and its delivery; the process is essentially revolutionary rather than evolutionary, an aim incompatible with most democratic and essentially conservative or centrist governments, and with the slow process of evolution in most education systems.

Identity is central to the way in which young people use the online world, but this does not necessarily mean they simply preserve and present their real-life (RL) identity in another environment. In many cases they present versions of the person they would like to be, or play the role of someone else completely. The government targets come closest to this area when they propose moving towards e-mail addresses for all students and teachers. The targets here have been very much taken over by events, however, especially that of an e-mail address for only 50 per cent of all students by 2002. Although no definitive studies are available, anecdotal evidence from a number of classrooms suggests that in many schools this has already been achieved and in others 100 per cent of students have e-mail addresses. The target was set at a time when Internet access and e-mail addresses were a bought commodity; by 2000 the market had gone through another cycle of change so that Internet Service Providers and e-mail addresses, especially those that are Web-based, were increasingly likely to be free at the point of delivery, and financed by advertising and the collection of market research data.

It is also debatable whether any student will want to use a government-provided e-mail address. At the time of writing there is considerable discussion of the form these might take, with the current favourite likely to lead to an e-mail address such as smitha@stjohnsce_primary.birmingham. sch.uk, with the lengthy domain name indicating school, lea and sector. This kind of email address is attractive to policy-makers to whom it is orderly, transparent and manageable; to many young people it will be an appalling and distinctly unattractive solution.

Even where young people have their own e-mail addresses they have begun to use forwarding addresses that are easier to remember, present the right image and provide the user with a measure of anonymity. We are told (Lee, 1996: 282) that short e-mail addresses have higher cachet than the longer cumbersome ones provided by some institutions and Internet Service Providers, an important message for the designers of the UK e-mail for all schools project. An address such as http://atschool.eduweb.co.uk/ cabbott/ can be replaced, apparently, by come.to/chrisabbott or some such address. The forwarding service achieves this by creating aliases which lead the software to the right destination by use of the numerical (IP) address which underlies all textual Internet addressing.

These changes are transitory; forwarding addresses are an online response to informal evaluation by young people, which leads to them using certain services and not others. Very soon, new versions of Web browsers may have their own built-in version of forwarding, and the forwarding agencies will then die, or reinvent themselves to meet needs current at that time. It is this state of permanent and extensive change to which it is extremely important for governments to respond in policies extending over five-year periods.

The connection between the oral and the written text is another issue which has been an ongoing area of academic interest. There is little atten-tion paid to this area in the UK targets, although it could be argued that the move from paper to electronic communication between government and schools is related. It is possible that the use of electronic mail and informa-tion delivery by government might lead to fewer phone calls and fewer letters, but I remain sceptical about this. The more important differences are in the nature of communication, rather than merely in the quantity of it.

The Rise of the Internet

As a user of e-mail since 1988, I believe it took me more than five years before I felt comfortable enough with the medium to begin radically to alter my ways of working; and I still consume as much paper as I always did. I do, however, make far fewer phone calls, and it may well be true that one effect of online targets in education will be to privilege the written at the expense of the oral. Secretarial skills such as punctuation, spelling and formal grammar may well become rather more important than they have been, and this would be an outcome not predicted or apparently expected in the targets, despite its appeal to large numbers of voters.

The government does appear to have recognised the phenomenon of cybercommunities, at least in the sense of communities of teachers, if not of students. The Virtual Teachers Centre, the first part of the NGfL to be implemented, contains a series of interactive forums for teachers to explore and debate issues. Unfortunately, like so many of these interactive communities designed for, rather than by, people, they seem remarkably under-used.

The UK government, like most other political leaderships, is very much concerned about ownership of information, as are the young people described here. Young people are concerned with breaking down barriers which deny them access to words, images or music, particularly the latter, since the MP3 format enables CD-quality music tracks to be downloaded from the Internet. Their political leaders are more likely to be worried about the law-breaking involved in this activity. Where young citizens may argue for a re-examination of the concept of ownership of words, images and music, their leaders are more likely to be expending large amounts of money and effort on the replication of previous gate-keeping technologies for the online world. An example would be the development of the watermark facility, a hidden piece of code embedded in a copyrighted image – much as its real-life counterpart is an image which can be revealed by holding a piece of paper to the light.

Another example from the field of video would be the regionalising of DVD, the new standard for providing full-length feature films on CDROM. Recognising that pricing structures will vary in different parts of the world, manufacturers, with the collusion of governments, have divided the world up into five regions and ensured that DVDs purchased in one region cannot be played in another. A rapid response from young users followed, led by the knowledge gained by playing different versions of the disks on a computer: PCs may be able to play all the versions, but the DVD players that connect to a television are specific to a region. Learning quickly, these users found that a variety of technologies was used to block undesired use, and several of these were quickly subverted by software fixes which appeared rapidly on the Internet. Other solutions required reversion to the arcane world of soldering irons and hot metal; it has been claimed that dropping one globule of solder on a particular part of the circuit board of a certain brand of player is enough to make it play DVDs from another region.

The rapid acquisition and distribution of collective learning such as this pays eloquent testimony to the Internet as a progenitor of situated learning. It may not, of course, be the kind of learning of which governments would approve, but it is certainly effective and popular. The challenge for governments is to harness this motivation and potential, and direct it towards aims which might be described as meeting the general approval of society. This will probably mean a diminishing of the range of literacy practices and learning collectives on the Web so that only those secretarial skills which are a by-product of these practices become key outcomes themselves. This is likely to increase the alienation felt by young people who see the ICT on offer in schools as vastly inferior to the ICT they see in their own lives and that of their friends.

In summary, the UK government targets recognise that the Internet offers opportunities for communication and for collective learning. The government has also begun to understand that there are complex issues developing here with relation to previous boundaries between written and oral texts. On the other hand, it has yet to recognise the extent to which the Internet and its associated technologies thrive on change rather than permanence, and that this environment is suffocated by any attempt to describe it, delineate it or fix it in time. Similarly, the government targets fail to recognise that creation of identity and adherence to a community are both central attractions for users of this technology. It is tempting to surmise that those responsible for setting the targets were not themselves experienced users of the technologies described. An example is the decision to aim for 50 per cent of all young people to be e-mail users. Any regular user of e-mail would know it is largely ineffective when only half of the possible recipients are linked up; it is only when everyone is a possible recipient and producer that practices change and new opportunities develop.

What is needed in the UK is not this list of worthy but often mismatched targets, but enabling legislation which will allow local bottom-up grids to be built by communities of users, much as some of the digital cities such as those which began in the Netherlands in the mid-1990s have been built. A touch of anarchy and rather less of the institutional and formal could create more than even the large sums of money currently being spent are capable of; but perhaps that would be too daunting a prospect for a centrist *fin de siècle* government.

Beyond schools, the ascendant online metaphor of recent years, the global village, has been supported by the tendency of text-based environments to point up similarities rather than differences. In the early 1990s, most Internet texts were in English and for the most part used words only, and it is easy to see how the dominant mode came to be one of uniting across borders and of seeing a conjoint future with nations united in a post-geographical age. However, events in the Balkans, in an ever more divided Belgium, in Northern Ireland, in Spain and not least in an increasingly devolved and divided UK continue to indicate the importance of geographical and cultural boundaries.

It has been suggested (Gibson, 1996) that classrooms are an inappropriate response to a technological age, and that books embody a sense of closure (Bolter, 1996; Ong, 1982) which is at odds with current and future needs. Ong's work, in particular, has been seen (Lippert, 1996) as part of a shift from a temporal to a spatial phenomenology of the word, by which I understand him to suggest that words stand for meanings which relate to the environments in which they are found, rather than having one meaning fixed on them for all time at the moment of their creation. Lee (1996) reminds us that we have become familiar with McLuhan-like notions of language changing when the mode of communication shifts.

'Electric language' (Heim and Poster, 1990) is often characterised as being a mode which has echoes of other communication devices, with e-mail often seen as being something between the language of a telephone call and that of a letter. Code-switching, a key concept in this area, is nothing new (Lee, 1996), with Mark Twain's novel *Huckleberry Finn* cited as an early example of this kind of alternation between the literate and the oral. *Huckleberry Finn*, published in 1884, is popularly supposed to have been the first novel written on a typewriter and is therefore seen by some writers as a bridgehead among literary artefacts.

End-of-century publications have tended to portray *fin de siècle* attitudes, with dire predictions either of the imminent collapse of the school system (Papert, 1996), or that the online world will suffer from terminal overload and that this will free us from the tyranny of cyberspace and help us regain our rightful position in the real world (Postman, 1995).

> What we need ... is a revolution, in sensibility as well as lifestyle, capable of freeing us from our overdependence on abstractions; a revolution capable of reconnecting us to essential things – the things ... that we can experience directly and for ourselves, not through the mediating influence of technology.
>
> (Slouka, 1996: 136)

As we enter a new century, this area has become much more complex. The easy availability of visual information, first in the form of still images and then of moving video, has begun to remind Web users of the essential differences and varieties of the world's people. Young people have felt torn by this issue, often anxious to preserve the culture of which they are a part, and yet also wanting to use English, the lingua franca of the Internet, to communicate with the greatest possible number of people and be part of worldwide youth culture, which is heavily influenced by the USA. It is for this reason that the English among many 'Englishes' which is most often used on the Web is one heavily influenced by the US vernacular form of the language. In other cultures, for example that of Bangalore, India (Chamberlain, 1999), the Internet and the use of English are together offering opportunities for communication which are breaking long-standing cultural and caste barriers.

The tensions related to the US domination of the Internet and the relative importance of American English on the World Wide Web are linked to concerns about the development of a multinational publishing industry which is also dominated by groups based in the USA. The rise to power of multinationals such as Microsoft, News International and Pearson has caused concerns which are similar to those more closely related to the Web, with the success of Amazon and other booksellers threatening the future existence of local bookshops.

It has been suggested that children today live in an electronic world which requires new responses and new forms of organisation and which leads to the conclusion that current school curricula are inappropriate (Smith and Curtin, 1998). On the other hand, we are reminded of what has been lost alongside what has been gained:

> We have liberated data, but in doing so we have also wreaked havoc upon context, which we might think of as home for data...

> A piece of data, of information, only becomes a piece of knowledge when it can be understood as the answer to a question.
>
> (Birkerts, 1998: 25)

Even those who tend to espouse new media only because of a supposed link to traditional literacy forms are suspicious of the easy claims that technology is erasing what has gone before: 'That the new media are destroying old skills and values chimes all too easily with a whole variety of traditional pessimisms from both left and right' (McCabe, 1998: 33).

Birkerts suggests that we seem to be valuing the ability to roam far and wide electronically, to combine 'externality with a sophisticated awareness of interconnectedness' (Birkerts, 1998: 24), and to undervalue the ability to immerse oneself fully in one isolated space.

The imminent arrival of streaming audio, already possible for many users, will be likely to lead to an explosion of languages on the Web. For the first time it will be as easy to publish a message in Gujarati as in English, as easy to put forward a point of view in Arabic as in American English – provided that it is expressed in spoken dialogue. Once it becomes possible to converse in full-motion video on a computer screen and to share documents which are being written easily and conveniently, pressure is likely to grow for alternative models of schooling. With predictions of the end of schooling (Papert, 1996) beginning to attract more interest even where they have been far from convincing to many, the time seems to be coming when a re-examination is needed of the current model of schooling, based as it is on the need to create a compliant, uniformly skilled workforce for the late Victorian labour market.

If the information employment market is to favour the individualist and the quirky, innovation and enterprise, and the New Work Order is to be the recipe for the future, then it may well be that schooling which at least in part takes place in the home or in small local drop-in centres could be the future of the service. Only a few governments, principally that of Singapore, have really attempted to redesign their education service to make use of technological possibilities: but others, such as the UK and some states in the USA and Australia, are now beginning to consider these possibilities. The proposed Learning Centres and lifetime Learning Accounts in the UK, together with the University for Industry, could be the beginning of a very new style and location of lifelong learning. During the Austen Project, on which she worked with Seymour Papert and John Berlow, Shelley Turkle was struck by the way in which 'the creation of a child programming culture created new relationships between students, teachers, and curriculum' (Turkle, 1984: 95). It is possible that some of the plans for the UK will lead to the creation of some of these new relationships.

It is clear, then, that the UK educational system will change considerably in the next few years as a result of the Internet; but I would assert that the more fundamental change will come about because of the way in which young people will view learning. We will see an increase in informal learning, a rapid development of modular routes and an increasing reliance on distance learning methodologies.

Lifelong learning, individual learning accounts and fast access to the Internet, together with persistent concerns about the effectiveness of a school system designed for the Victorian workforce, lead to the possibility of demands for much more fundamental change. The activities of young men and women on the Internet raise serious questions about the future of schools. By 1998, Georgia Technological University estimated 38 per cent of Internet users in the USA to be female. The developed world is going online – and it is beginning to wonder if home-schooling might be nearer to the model of education for the future than a three-storey building in an inner-city full of a thousand disaffected adolescents throughout the school day and empty in the evening and during weekends and school holidays. Alternatives to schooling are once more on the agenda, as a response to a development which is as elusive to pin down as it is impossible to ignore.

the development of the new media – particularly the digitised multi-media of the CDROM, the Internet and the World Wide Web – has created a new form, one with which we are just beginning to come to terms, and one which – each time we seek to grasp it – eludes us, much as a jellyfish might elude a spear-fisher. The centre of learning appears to have vanished into cyberspace.

(Purves, 1998: 10)

In the twenty-first century, if we are to educate our young people effectively, efficiently and in a manner which gains their confidence and interest, we need to do so from a standpoint which indicates that we have learnt from them. To continue to pretend that nothing has changed, to wallow in a nostalgia for an educational past which never existed, and to refuse to recognise what has gone for ever as well as welcoming the exciting possibilities opening up before us, would be to miss one of the greatest opportunities education has ever been offered: an opportunity which is already being embraced by the young people who we assume need us in order to educate them. We examine these issues more fully in the next and final chapter.

Chapter Summary

- The public response to the Internet has been one of extremes: either wild unsubstantiated claims or blanket denials of relevance.
- Early responses to the Internet were related more to its effect on paper-based media than to the new features it might offer.
- The last five years have seen many countries competing to set ICT-related targets for schools and to connect them to the Internet.
- Only a few of these programmes, including that in the UK, have recognised the importance of teacher education.
- Government policies on Internet use are unlikely to match the fluid and developing mores of the system as created by its users.
- Issues of language and culture are thrown into relief by the Internet.
- Currently seen as a text-based medium, the Internet will become increasingly a medium of sound and moving image.

Bibliography

Abbott, C. (1994). *Reading IT*. Reading: University of Reading.
Becker, H. J. and Ravitz, J. L. (1998). The equity threat of promising innovations: pioneering internet-connected schools. *Journal of Educational Computing Research*, 19(1), 1–26.

Bier, M., Gallo, M., Nucklos, E., Sherblom, S. and Pennick, M. (1997). Personal empowerment in the study of home Internet use by low-income families. *Journal of Research on Computing in Education*, 30(2), 107–21.

Birkerts, S. (1998). The implications of virtuality. In B. Cox (ed.), *Literacy is Not Enough* (18–28). Manchester: Manchester University Press/Book Trust.

Boal, I. A. (1995). A flow of monsters: Luddism and virtual technologies. In J. Brook and I. A. Broal (eds.), *Resisting the Virtual Life* (3–16). San Francisco: City Lights Books.

Bolter, J. D. (1991). *Writing Space; The Computer, Hypertext and the History of Writing*. Hillsdale, NJ: Lawrence Erlbaum.

—— (1996). Virtual reality and the redefinition of self. In L. Strate (ed.), *Communications in Cyberspace* (105–20). Cresskill, NJ: Hampton Press.

Brown, P. and Levinson, S. (1987). *Politeness: Some Universals in Language Usage*. Cambridge: Cambridge University Press.

Chamberlain, S. (1999). Single male seeks sexy chatty online. *The Daily Telegraph – Connected*, 25 March, 4–5.

Coupland, D. (1995). *Microserfs*. London: Flamingo.

Cox, M. J. (1993). Technology enriched school project – the impact of information technology on children's learning. *Computers and Education*, 21 (1/2), 41–9.

Dannatt, A. (1992). The book that ate itself. *The Independent*, 19 December.

DfEE (1997). *Connecting the Learning Society*. London: HMSO.

Drew, J. (1995). Media Activism and Radical Democracy. In J. Brook and I. A. Broal (eds.), *Resisting the Virtual Life* (71–84). San Francisco: City Lights Books.

Fielding, H. (1994). Screen secrets: an office user's guide. *The Independent*, January.

Gates, B. (1999). *Business Using a Digital Nervous System*. London: Penguin.

Gibson, S. B. (1996). Pedagogy and Hypertext. In L. Strate (ed.), *Communications and Cyberspace* (243–60). Cresskill, NJ: Hampton Press.

Gorard, S. and Selwyn, N. (1999). Switching on the learning society? Questioning the role of technology in widening participation in lifelong learning. *Journal of Education Policy*, 14 (5), 523–34.

Heim, M. (1993). *The Metaphysics of Virtual Reality*. Oxford: Oxford University Press.

Heim, M. and Poster, M. (1990). *The Mode of Information: Poststructuralism and Social Context*. Chicago: University of Chicago Press.

Kress, G. and Van Leeuwen, T. (1996). *Reading Images: The Grammar of Visual Design*. London: Routledge.

Lee, J. Y. (1996). Charting the codes of cyberspace: a rhetoric of electronic mail. In L. Strate (ed.), *Communications and Cyberspace* (275–96). Cresskill, NJ: Hampton Press.

Lippert, P. J. (1996). Cinematic representations of cyberspace. In L. Strate (ed.), *Communications and Cyberspace* (261–70). Cresskill, NJ: Hampton Press.

McCabe, C. (1998). Television and literacy. In B. Cox (ed.), *Literacy is Not Enough* (29–40). Manchester: Manchester University Press/Book Trust.

Miller, L. (1995). Women and children first: gender and the settling of the electronic frontier. In J. Brook and I. A. Broal (eds), *Resisting the Virtual Life* (49–58). San Francisco: City Lights Books.

Ong, W. J. (1982). *Orality and Literacy*. London: Methuen.

Papert, S. (1996). *The Connected Family: Bridging the Generation Gap*. Atlanta, GA: Longstreet Press.

Postman, N. (1995). *The End of Education: Redefining the Value of School*. New York: Alfred A. Knopf.

Purves, A. C. (1998). *The Web of Text and the Web of God*. London: The Guilford Press.

Reddy, M. (1979). The conduit metaphor. In A. Ortony (ed.), *Metaphor and Thought*. Cambridge: Cambridge University Press.

Sefton-Green, J. (ed.). (1999). *Young People, Creativity and the New Technologies*. London: Routledge.

Selwyn, N. (1997). The continuing weakness of educational computing research. *British Journal of Educational Computing*, 28 (4), 305–7.

—— (1998). A grid for learning or a grid for earning? The significance of the Learning Grid initiative in UK education. *Journal of Education Policy*, 13 (3), 423–31.

Slouka, M. (1996). *War of the Worlds: the Assault on Reality*. London: Abacus.

Smith, R. and Curtin, P. (1998). Computers and life online: education in a cyber-world. In I. Snyder (ed.), *Taking Literacy into the Electronic Age*. Sydney: Allen & Unwin.

Stoll, C. (1995). *Silicon Snake Oil: Second Thoughts on the Information Superhighway*. London: Macmillan.

Street, B. (1988). Literary practices and literacy myths. In R. Saljo (ed.), *The Written Word: Studies in Literate Thought and Action* (vol. 23, 59–72). Heidelberg: Springer-Verlag.

Sutcliffe, T. (1993). Happiness is :) in baudy language. *The Independent*, 4 November

Turkle, S. (1984). *Second Self: Computers and the Human Spirit*. New York: Simon & Schuster.

Watson, D. (ed.) (1993). *The Impact Report: An Evaluation of the Impact of Information Technology on Children's Achievements in Primary and Secondary Schools*. London: DES and King's College London.

7 Towards a New Understanding of ICT and Schools

The landscape of discussion inhabited by ICT is changing all the time, and there are welcome signs of increasing maturity in what has often been previously a strident and superficial discourse. Thoughtful studies of the role and functions of the Internet within society in general are beginning to appear (Slevin, 2000). In his book, Slevin answers some of the previous debates and does much to link together the varied aspects of globalisation and the changing nation state. His comments on human interaction online, in particular, have much to say that might be considered by educationists and policy makers. In particular, he warns of the possibility that the relative freedom of access and opinion currently enjoyed online may be a transitory and temporary phase.

> the idea of democratization, and thereby the revitalization of community, is a problematic one. Guaranteeing the rights of members of a community to free speech and free association, for example, has never led to the successful creation of community. Without some kind of balance between individual freedoms on the one hand and responsibilities for issues on the other, any sense of community may soon evaporate, like Lyotard's cloud, in the heat of the moment.
>
> (Slevin, 2000: 99)

Slevin argues throughout his book for online practices to be examined within the social and historical contexts from which they have arisen, a concern which I share and which I have attempted to meet in this study. He argues that the effect of online practices on modern culture can only be understood if the Internet is studied as a 'contextualised social phenomenon' (Slevin, 2000: 28). Slevin is unconvinced by arguments that the Internet has removed concepts of time and place, and he asserts that those who are actors within virtual reality scenarios are also situated in a reality which is relevant and worthy of understanding. Unlike other commentators, Slevin sees the Internet and its denizens as characteristic of late modernity rather than being linked to a post-modern view of the world.

ICT and National Policies – Some Current Initiatives

At a time of growing understanding of the extent of the change caused by ICT, the following conference announcement indicates some of the areas that concern researchers in this field.

> The last few years have seen a burgeoning awareness of the potential impact of new electronic technologies. We now recognise the crucial need to understand the social circumstances which can realise techno-logical benefits, to temper cyberbole with sober social scientific research. Frameworks have been developed to help us ask: to what extent are significant changes in the ways we interact, relate to each other and organise ourselves associated with the new technologies? So what now are the prospects for a 'virtual society'? Are we now at the point where we might consider removing the question mark? Should we replace it with an exclamation mark! Or should we now redouble our analytic scepticism?
>
> (Virtual-Society, 2000)

The domain referred to here is the wider one of society in general, but it is within the educational system that most of the research is taking place and on which much of it is focused.

Within national educational systems the prime motivator, at least for politicians, all too often seems to be that of seeking to be the best country or the top country or the most connected country. The UK targets for 2002 have already been described, and these are in many ways among the most far-reaching and ambitious of the current period. However, most countries have attempted to address this area in differing ways and to different extents.

ICT Policies and the European Union

The provision of some kind of electronic network for schools has been the most obvious activity for many nation states, especially those in the European Union. The European Schoolnet (http://www.eun.org) has been a driving force here, as have the wider activities in this area of the European Union. In late 1999, European Schoolnet published a summary of *Technology in Education in Europe* (http://www.en.eun.org/news/ictdev/ictdev.html).

The report contains overviews of the role of ICT in education around Europe and the first phase of results, based on questionnaires sent to senior policy makers. The report outlines general statistics and figures about the use of the Internet, the numbers of students per computer, the standards in hardware, the percentage of schools connected to the Net, public expenditure on resources and competences in ICT in schools. This first report covered Denmark, Belgium, Finland, Germany, Luxembourg, Portugal and Sweden.

The report places European developments within a worldwide context and suggests that the current position in which 42 per cent of the world's Internet users are in Europe will change so that by 2005 non-US users in Europe and elsewhere will account for 70 per cent of users. This raises an interesting issue, especially for those countries who have been concerned at what they see as the domination by the USA of online life. If their predictions are correct, Americans online will become a minority within a few years. It is, however, notoriously difficult to make predictions in this area – without predicting the invention of the silicon chip no one could have foreseen the rapid home ownership of computers, and there may be similar unexpected developments in the next few years.

Since the report is concerned with education it looks next at the number of students per computer in each of the European countries studied. Unfortunately, not all the countries involved have collected such figures, but the variation is clearly a wide one. For primary schools, at the most well-equipped end of the range come countries such as the UK, with thirteen pupils per computer, and Finland, with twelve. At the other extreme Italy has a ratio of 1:28.5 and Portugal only has one computer for each 150 pupils, although the ratio is much better there in secondary schools. Further analysis focuses on the type of computer available; many of these statistics mean little without this extra information, since a five-year-old computer may be of no real use. Some research (Alspaugh, 1999) has also shown that there may be no relationship between educational outcomes and the computer–student ratio in the classroom.

The target computer–student ratios for each country are interesting and worth further consideration. Six of the countries studied, in addition to the UK, have targets for ICT use. In Denmark, the emphasis is on primary schools, with a target ratio by 2003 of something between 1:5 and 1:10, where these computers are less than five years old. Belgium, or at least the Flemish part of that increasingly divided country, has a target ratio of 1:10 in all schools by 2002. In Finland, no target date is set but the ratios aimed at are 1:10 in primary and 1:7 in secondary education. The only German target announced is to connect all schools to the Internet; with its federal structure Germany has seen little in the way of national projects in this area although some Länder are now making progress with developing the infrastructure in their area. In Portugal, target ratios by 2003 are to be 1:25 in primary schools, 1:20 in secondary schools, and 1:10 at all levels by 2006.

It is interesting to note that the UK, one of the first European countries to move to a targeted approach in this area, has targets for almost everything except the teacher–computer ratio. The UK targets, as will be discussed later, are related as much to British aspirations as they are to educational development. Also very different are the Swedish targets, which relate to equality for all pupils, as well as training for teachers. The very different UK and Swedish ICT policy documents will be discussed below.

The European Schoolnet report goes on to discuss the percentage of schools connected to the Internet in each country, and recognises that this is approaching 100 per cent for secondary schools in more than half of the countries studied. The percentage of schools with high speed (ISDN or leased line) connections is lower in most countries, although Denmark and Finland have made considerable progress in this area and the vast majority of school Internet connections in those countries are at faster rates.

Using the common Euro currency as the point of comparison, the resources put in to this area by each country are compared. It is difficult to draw any conclusions, as some figures are gross and others relate to expenditure per pupil. Only four of the countries studied were willing to answer the question about plans for training teachers (Sweden, Finland, Italy and the Netherlands) and very few countries were willing to assess the number of their teachers with basic competence in ICT. Again, the Nordic countries tended to score highest here. Asked about the percentage of students using ICT regularly, only Sweden and Italy answered, with a remarkable difference between the answers: in Sweden 20 per cent of students use ICT every day, while in Italy only 2 per cent do so.

Activity

The picture emerging, at least from this survey of some of the countries in Europe, is that of a highly developed Nordic sector, a reasonably well-developed northern European area and a broad swathe of southern Europe where much remains to be done.

Is this simply a reflection of comparative prosperity, or do you think other factors affect aspirations in this area? Does geography play a part? Or history? Or politics?

The Council of Europe has published a declaration (Committee of Ministers, 1999) regarding a European policy on information technologies. The declaration was produced at a meeting in Budapest which marked the fiftieth anniversary of the Council of Europe. The statement begins with a series of statements recognising the difficulties surrounding this area, but then goes on to charge member states to consider two broad areas as they develop their policies: diversity of content and language and protection of rights and freedoms.

The European Commission (EC), on the other hand, has put most of its efforts into issues of access and equality. In early 2000, the Commission produced a report called *Tomorrow's Education: Promoting Innovation with New Technologies* (http://www.en.eun.org/news/designingtomorrowseducation.html). This report outlined some key areas of development across Europe. It is considerably more detailed than the European Schoolnet report and looks more closely at policy instead of examining current targets. Sections of the report look at matching technology to practice, the conditions which help ICT use to thrive and the priorities for the future. The report is part of an EC policy of moving towards a common policy in this area. The point is made early in the report that much of the equipping phase has now passed and the issues now facing many countries are those of implementation, practice and innovation.

In what could be seen as a typically Commission-based approach, the first section of the report considers what it sees as the difficulties of merging practice and technology at a time when priorities are so different in various countries. It goes on to call for 'ambitious initiatives' if this area is to be adequately addressed.

The next section of the report describes the arrival of multimedia and the Internet as the 'start of a new era'. It contrasts the rapid development in this area with that of education, which it sees as a much more long-term process. The call here is for consistent strategies over time. The arrival of the World Wide Web is seen as a defining moment and the rapid development of online visual and auditory resources is examined as an indication of the need for improved access rates. It is recognised that, although the Web may offer immediacy and quantity, education needs 'quality and consistency'.

An interesting dichotomy explored in this section is the existence of much of the most innovative ICT use in the primary sector, even though in the majority of European countries past support and emphasis has been on secondary schools. The report suggests that this innovation arises from the typical primary setting in which education is more pupil-centred than it is in the later years. It sees ICT in use during the primary phase not only for education but also linked to what it describes as the 'functions of socialisation'. The report notes the remarkable persistence of the innovative small rural school in ICT projects, a presence far in excess of what would be expected proportionately. The section ends by making the sobering point that little real change in practice can be expected unless the external assessment tools, the examination systems, lead this change.

Reference is made to the differing picture across European countries, but it is considered that ICT practice in the continent's schools holds up well against the generality of what can be found in the USA. Where the

USA does have a clear lead is in the use of ICT in higher and post-university education, where much of Europe is still only at pilot and experimental stages.

When discussing the need for action by public authorities, the EC report calls attention to the numerous projects it has funded, including the Telematics, Socrates and Leonardo schemes. The report is one of the first to recognise that there may be a desired maximum number of PCs in a classroom and that this would not be as high as one per student. It suggests that the rapid expansion in home ownership will enable schools to see their role in the provision of ICT as a partner in the educational process rather than as the sole provider.

A useful appendix to the report lists ICT initiatives across Europe which were current in early 2000. The UK move from Superhighways Initiative (Scrimshaw, 1997) to the launch of the National Grid for Learning and its associated targets (DfEE, 1997) is cited as a good example of the way in which many countries have moved from a pilot to an implementation stage.

By nature tending to be bland and consensual, EC documents sometimes run the risk of appearing to see all countries in Europe through the same, possibly slightly rose-tinted, spectacles. An examination of two very different policy documents for ICT in education, that for Sweden and the plan for UK which has already been discussed, will indicate some of the tensions and differences which exist at the political and social levels.

A Comparison of Two Policy Documents: The UK and Sweden

It is an indication of the political importance of the UK document, *Connecting the Learning Society* (DfEE, 1997), that it begins with a Foreword by Prime Minister Tony Blair. The first line of this Foreword includes the phrase 'helping our businesses to compete' and it is clear throughout the document that the agenda is one of rising above the competition rather than seeking to work with others. ICT skills in young people are to be lifted to the 'level of the best in the world'.

The Foreword goes on to link the two hurdles it claims need to be overcome: training teachers to use ICT and creating a market for high-quality British educational software. While these might both be quite laudable aims – and the UK does have a range of innovative software products – this is a surprising coupling in a report of this nature and is not mirrored in any of the other European policy documents. It appears that only the UK, among European countries, wants to win this particular race.

The development of the Grid envisaged in the report is also closely tied in to the development of public/private partnerships (PPP), a key government policy. The development of competing managed services is seen as the way forward that is most likely to lead to consistent and appropriate support for ICT in education. By mid-2000 there had certainly been developments in this area but progress towards any major move in the direction of PPP for ICT seemed to be slow and unclear. Meanwhile, other governments such as that of the Flemish community in Belgium began to develop their own PPP projects in the area of ICT and education.

The cover of the UK document conveys a discreet but important message. As a discreet caption inside makes clear, the small images featured are of 'communications technology over four millennia, from hieroglyphs, manuscript and movable type, to digital computing'. The images are powerful and reassuring ones, linking ICT by direct linear sequence with the historically highly valued technologies of print- and word-based communication. The use of the phrase 'Learning Society' in the title is interesting too, and reminds the reader of a previous prime minister, Margaret Thatcher, who claimed that there was no such thing as society. The notion of a Learning Society is closely linked to other New Labour policies and stances.

If the key message of *Connecting the Learning Society* is that the UK will be the best and will overtake all the others, the impression given by *Tools for Learning IT* (Ministry for Education and Science, 1998), the Swedish policy document, is very different. This document too begins with a Foreword by a minister, in this case the Minister for Schools and Adult Education Ylva Johansson. She begins by placing communication at the centre of ICT, and this focus continues throughout the document. She states quite unequivocally that this technology can never replace schools or teachers and then goes on to raise what she sees as the key issue: equality of access. Rather than seeking to be better or more successful than anyone else, the Swedish approach is to use the technology to make contact with others.

> ICT can also open up schools to the outside world. Today, teachers and pupils in different countries can make direct contact and thereby generate new, instructive discussions and new contacts. Frontierless conversations are within reach of more people than ever.
>
> (Ministry for Education and Science, 1998: 3)

Where the British publication used illustrations only of print and other technology, the Swedish document uses coloured photographs throughout of active, enquiring Swedish schoolchildren. Only three of these pictures include a computer, and even then in two out of the three the computer is an insignificant part of the overall image. The emphasis is clear: this is a document about people not about technology.

The report talks about the knowledge society, a similar concept to that of the UK learning society, especially allowing for the difficulty of translation; the Swedish document was published in English as well as Swedish.

An important area covered in the Swedish document and omitted entirely from the UK one is that of the school environment and ICT. In every Swedish school district, ergonomists supervise the working environment and ensure that health and safety issues are addressed. Some of the supervision in this area is undertaken by pupil safety representatives. The role of women is discussed in the document, and the continuing need to challenge the historically-privileged role of men in this area is indicated alongside some challenging assertions.

> Girls are interested in seeing context and meaning. They regard technology as a means to this or that end. Boys, on the other hand, more often see technology as having intrinsic value. ...

> The main thrust of policy must therefore be to give women access to technology on their own terms. Arousing women's interest in the use of computers thus requires more effort than arousing men's. It is also important to work for a massive change in the culture that has previously prevailed in ICT contexts. Only then can ICT attract both sexes on equal terms.
> (Ministry for Education and Science, 1998: 14)

There are echoes here of the argument (Spender, 1995) that for women technology must offer communication, and that the telephone is the device with which many women are most comfortable, but the stance is not one that is universally held. We are reminded also of suggestions (Millard, 1997) that boys read for factual information whereas girls tend to seek to understand and recognise relationships in their reading, and of the fact that what schools do is of significance in the attitudes that boys take to their learning (Head, 1999). Head's discussion of the difficulties that boys have in acknowledging their own worries and concerns is very relevant to any examination of online practice. Even the most cursory attendance in some of the online chat rooms apparently frequented by young males indicates the considerable anxiety and feelings of inadequacy apparent in the utterances of these participants. They constantly seek the approval of their peers, check that their experiences are shared by others and seek to conform to the norm wherever it is possible to do so.

The Swedish document goes on to talk about other areas that do not feature in the British plan. The potential of ICT to provide new opportunities for democratic involvement is discussed, as is the possibility of linking together those young people who live in less populated areas.

Sweden has a particularly impressive history of supporting pupils with special educational needs (SEN) by using ICT, and the report notes that every pupil with visual impairment or severe motor disabilities now has a computer. Much of the work that has achieved this enviable state of affairs has gone on at the Swedish National Agency for Special Needs Education (SIH), a world-leading organisation in this area (http://www.sih.se/engelsk/indexeng.htm). It is interesting to note that this track record is noted rather than celebrated in the report, and indeed SIH continues to invite visitors from other European countries to its annual and very influential ID-Days rather than seeking to tell others how they should be supporting this area or promoting Sweden as the world leader it undoubtedly is where SEN and ICT are concerned.

It is relevant here to note that the world ICT-SEN community is an increasingly connected one which has made good use of the potential of the technologies for connecting people as well as for supporting learners. Major exhibitions and conferences in this area, such as Closing the Gap in the USA or the ID-Days event in Sweden mentioned above, have brought together practitioners from around the world. The best of these events have also made it possible for all those involved – clients, carers, teachers, therapists and parents – to meet together in an open and productive dialogue. Once again, the potential of the Internet for supporting minority groups is underlined by this development, as has been shown by the two research projects I have led in this area at King's College (http://www.sed.kcl.ac.uk/special/). These projects were supported by the Viscount Nuffield Auxiliary Fund.

Perhaps most surprisingly of all, the Swedish Report ends with several pages describing the developments going on in Norway, Denmark, Finland and the UK. It would be hard to imagine a British policy document including the progress made by other countries in this way.

ICT: Changing Education? What School Might Become

> The disestablishment of schools will inevitably happen ... (but) it could take place in either of two diametrically opposed ways.
>
> The first would be the expansion of the mandate of the pedagogue and his increasing control over society even outside school. ... Deschooling, which we cannot stop, could mean the advent of a 'brave new world' dominated by well-intentioned administrators of programmed instruction.
>
> On the other hand, the growing awareness ... that graded curricular teaching for certification has become harmful could offer large masses of people an extraordinary opportunity: that of preserving the right of equal access to the tools both of learning and of sharing with others what they know or believe.
>
> (Illich, 1973: 104)

When Illich made his far-ranging criticisms of the school system and predicted its imminent collapse in the light of its perceived inappropriateness, he was widely pilloried for what were seen at the time as extreme and inappropriate views. However, the predictions he made almost thirty years ago now seem much less extreme, as more and more mainstream writers recognise that, to some extent, education is changing as it has never changed before. Even as practical a publication as a handbook for senior managers in schools can include statements which would have seemed startling as little as ten years ago:

> We have all already witnessed some of the significant social and economic consequences of ... IT and its impact on education. It is only possible to guess at a future when the whole process of schooling will be transformed, particularly as technologies which shift the focus and choice of the curriculum to the learner are further developed.
>
> (Donnelly, 1998: 8)

One of the perennial problems in the area of technological change in schools is the understandable temptation to write about the future before we fully understand the present. Of course, there will never be a right time to look forward, any more than there is ever a right time to buy a computer; both activities will be rendered out of date as soon as they are completed. Attempts have been made in recent years to look at the area of technology and how it is changing schools (Tiffin and Rajasingham, 1995), and even those few years ago it was very difficult to foresee, for example, the rise of the Web.

Tiffin and Rajasingham gathered together a range of ideas in their book, which was based on their experiences in New Zealand, a country whose education system is much less familiar to European or US readers than their own. Their starting point is their belief, shared with many others, that we are moving from an industrial to an information society. Their answer is to propose a new model of schooling more suited to the current age than one based, as they rightly point out, on the needs of an industrially based work order. This is not to suggest that they argue for a replacement of teacherly contact; quite the reverse, for they recognise the essential social role of much learning. Their argument is for a technologically rich learning centre, which uses virtual reality to build on the possibilities of current classrooms, teachers and learners.

Tiffin and Rajasingham recognise that education is essentially about communication, as are many of the technologies now found in our schools and homes. They are aware of the importance of networking, in both its technological and social senses.

Today, people accept limitations on what they learn because of where they live. The virtual class opens the possibility that any learner, no matter where they are, could be put in touch with any teacher, in any area of knowledge, that addresses any problem domain. Although conventional classes will continue for some things, they will co-exist with virtual classes.

(Tiffin and Rajasingham, 1995: 162)

Postman (1971) gave some indication of a future role for a city school if it were to become more of a socio-political community base. He describes the services such a school might provide as including community services, household goods servicing, cultural services, sports facilities and work for city agencies (Postman and Weingartner, 1971). With the arrival of computers and the linked reprographic facilities that exist in all schools, there is clearly considerable potential for a shift along these lines, and much of this development has already begun in the UK.

More recently, Postman (1995) has returned to this topic and attempted once more to define what he sees as the value of schooling. In a chapter pithily entitled 'Some new gods that fail', he describes the claims made for technology as being insupportable in many cases. The limitations of his argument are that it is based on one country's educational system, that of the USA, and one notion of what education is all about. This is clear in the following paragraph:

In all strands of American cultural life, one can find so many examples of technological adoration that it is possible to write a book about it. ... But nowhere do you find more enthusiasm for the god of Technology than among educators. In fact, there are those, like Lewis Perelman, who argue (for example, in his book *School's Out*) that modern information technologies have rendered schools entirely irrelevant, since there is now much more information available outside the classroom than inside.

(Postman, 1995: 38)

The limitations of this argument are that it relates fundamentally to American ideas about cultural life and about education, ideas which may not hold sway in much of the rest of the world. Technological adoration, for example, has been much less apparent in many European countries than it has in the more consumerist society of the USA. More fundamentally, the information transmission model of education which underlies Postman's assumptions is not acceptable or accurate when applied to education in much of Europe.

Postman's rejection of technology is based on his quite correct assumption that computers cannot replace teachers. He seems much less aware that radical change could follow from technology developing as a supporting tool for learning, just as teachers are increasingly seen as knowledgeable guides for learners rather than as the fount of all knowledge to be poured into their pupils.

> I do not go as far back as the introduction of the radio and the Victrola, but I am old enough to remember when sixteen-millimetre film was to be the sure cure; then closed-circuit television, then eight-millimetre film, then teacherproof text-books. Now computers.
>
> I know a false god when I see one.
>
> (Postman, 1995: 38)

The point made would be a valid one if informed educationists were really suggesting that computers are some kind of cure, or a fix which would turn mediocre teachers into great ones. In fact, no one with any real understanding of the field is making such claims, although they could be heard in earlier years. Computers are not a medical cure to be prescribed or a mediating agent to change teachers; they are tools to support learning and learners.

More recently, the British Computer Society (BCS) published a report (Passey, 1998) examining the school of the future in a UK context. The report makes use of words familiar from the cyberbole discussed earlier, with 'revolution' and 'the future' much in evidence. The document is described as an interactive one, a living document which will be re-issued in later amended versions. By mid-2000, however, contributions were still being sought for these and no further version had been issued.

One of the most forward-thinking Local Education Authority (LEA) Chief Education Officers, Tim Brighouse in Birmingham, has already begun the transformation of that large Midlands authority. In his Moray House lecture in Edinburgh in 1999, Brighouse outlined some of the changes, and they were reiterated in a version of the speech printed in *The Independent*. He wrote that he expected great changes in Birmingham by 2020: secondary education, in particular, would have been transformed. He predicted the end of what he termed the metronomic timetable, a timetable which insists on evenly spaced, even-length subject lessons taking place to a prepared plan. The curriculum, Brighouse suggests, will be individualised by 2020 and the school will give over as much as six weeks of the year to 'non-metronomic' activities, which might be mixed age.

All this has come from a man who could never be described as a technocrat. When giving a keynote speech at the IFTE (International Federation of Teachers of English) Conference in Birmingham in 1999 he famously used the provided computer and presentation software as a combined arm-rest and lectern, illustrating his talk with handwritten overheads.

The Birmingham plan uses the analogy of a wheel:

> We are even now planning a 'hub' and 'spokes' – a broad-based network among groups of a dozen secondary schools to create learning centres in a city to be run in a way that evokes master classes, research projects for the academically gifted, and after-school and before-school supplementary lessons through video links and distance tutors.
>
> (Brighouse, 1999)

Brighouse sees two other aspects as being essential for these changes: the first is enlightened use of the planned University of the First Age, the second the virtual school or college for those disaffected from the mainstream system. Although he speaks for an urban authority, Brighouse sees the need for these changes in rural areas too, although not perhaps with the same urgency. He is an optimist and ends his article by suggesting that those who come after us will 'wonder at the limit of our expectations and the modesty of our reach' (Brighouse, 1999). The Birmingham approach has attracted a good deal of attention from central government, and in early 2000 Doug Brown, a key adviser on the Birmingham Grid and also involved in the BCS report already discussed, was appointed to lead the National Grid for Learning Team at the DfEE.

Another conservative body, the Royal Society of Arts, proposed wide-ranging changes in its report which, importantly, was entitled *Redefining Schooling* (Bayliss, 1999). In her report for the RSA, Bayliss, herself a former head of youth and education policy at the DfEE, urges schools to open all the year round and to make it possible for pupils to work to timetables individually negotiated with their parents and teachers. The report calls for children to be actively accessing information in school rather than passively absorbing knowledge, and to see their teachers as co-enquirers and guides rather than as the fount of all knowledge. The key drive of the report is to persuade those in the education system to value skills and competence as well as the possession of information.

Real change is already happening in some schools in the UK. The definitive text on current Internet use in UK secondary schools (Grey, 1999) has been written not by a university academic but by a practising teacher. Grey's book is a very welcome compendium of wise words, sensible advice and careful forward thinking. An English and IT teacher, he begins his book with a compelling vision of a vacuum cleaner on the library roof, sucking in all the information which he may need to use and transform with his students. By the second page, he is reassuring his reader.

> This is not a threatening technical book. You should find it in the education section of your bookshop not the computer section. It does

not support any one computer platform over another or argue the case for one piece of software over another. In fact I would say that the Internet has made much of that old argument redundant.

(Grey, 1999: 2)

It is clear that the argument has moved on and matured; we are no longer dealing with the hype and its opposite, but with the measured, thoughtful deliberations of skilled practitioners. In Grey's book – supported of course by a linked Web site – we find a vision which can evolve from where we are now and which does not involve abandoning what is working in favour of untried alternatives. Grey looks ahead too, although he recognises the risks of doing so, especially in a printed book which can be consulted again in years to come. He recognises the major role to be played by sound and moving images in the future, and that it is essential that teachers have their own computers. School buildings, Grey believes, may come to be less important as sites of learning.

Increasingly we will move away from the four closed walls of the classroom. Joining the community around the school moves these walls, but also barriers of time and place are erased by technology. ...

Given skilled teachers and effective and available technology, teaching in a classroom could be an option but not a necessity. ...

(Grey, 1999: 133)

Grey goes on to describe a four-stage model of moving towards a virtual classroom. This can be summarised as:

Stage 1   Open-plan learning across classrooms and library.
Stage 2   Dropping the timetable for a fixed period.
Stage 3   Split day with traditional and open learning.
Stage 4   Real individual learning, supervised by tutor.

(Summarised from Grey, 1999: 134–5)

One of the major attractions of this model is its evolutionary nature. In the mature stage of discussion which ICT in education is now reaching, it is increasingly recognised that the way forward is more likely to be through small but important steps than by wholesale dramatic changes. Grey teaches in a secondary school, and it is in the upper end of the secondary school that this evolutionary change is likely to happen first, led by such innovative teachers, librarians and school managers. Some of those innovative teachers may find their ways of working and their relationships with their pupils changing as a result of these developments. One way in which this might happen is by the setting up of a new paradigm of the teacher, such as the PET or Peripatetic Electronic Teacher (Squires, 1999). Squires put forward his proposal as applicable within a higher-education setting but much of what he describes could develop within the school sector.

Open learning centres have become an important part of further and adult education in the UK, and ICT will enable these approaches to be offered to a much wider range of learners, especially those in secondary school. The growing acceptance of lifelong learning as a worldwide concept makes it ever more likely that education will no longer be a one-off opportunity which, if lost, can never be continued at a later stage.

A British newspaper (O'Sullivan, 2000) has described just such an experiment in one of the newer unitary authorities in the UK. The article announced that Britain's first cyber-school would open in August 2000 when Scottish pupils returned to their schools in Alloa, Clackmanannshire. The plan was for pupils to spend half a day a week in an open learning centre using technology to study the subjects of history, geography, science and technology. Clackmannanshire gave the title 'learning plaza' to this open learning site and provided thirty-two computers, a video suite and virtual learning technology. A cybercafe was attached and there were long-term plans to study other subjects in this way.

Ken Bloomer, Director of Education for the county, was confident in his claims of a pedagogical base for these actions. 'Research is showing us that children's brains do not function like calculators, learning in a logical sequence', he is reported (O'Sullivan, 2000) to have said; 'we now realise that pupils are good at taking information from lots of different sources and making sense of it'. The Clackmannanshire plan is derived from a Californian model used in San Diego. The county has indicated that it sees the system as a possible way forward for the secondary sector in general, although Bloomer agrees with many others in feeling that the primary school, on the other hand, is valid in its current state. He joins the voices of those many others calling for a leaner, more community-based and flex-ible secondary sector.

> Obviously a lot – such as the social experience of school – could be lost if everyday learning was simply done individually. But if the purpose of school buildings is principally going to be about personal growth and development, then perhaps that could be done better in smaller, more local situations.
>
> (Bloomer quoted in O'Sullivan, 2000)

Literacy, too, is changing and become more complex. Young learners are already learning to cope with an increasingly complex and multimedia-enriched world, and educational environments and tools will need to take account of this. We are finally recognising that some of what we read in the 1960s and dismissed as being hopelessly overstated may in fact show more insight than we expected, whether that be in Illich's provocative proposals or in the more learner-centred writing of John Holt:

> Behind much of what we do in school lie some ideas, that could be expressed as follows: (1) Of the vast body of human knowledge, there are certain bits and pieces that can be called essential, that everyone should know; (2) the extent to which a person can be considered educated, qualified to live intelligently in today's world and be a useful member of society, depends on the amount of this essential knowledge that he carries about with him [sic]; (3) it is the duty of schools, therefore, to get as much of this essential knowledge as possible into the minds of children. Thus we find ourselves trying to poke certain facts, recipes and ideas down the gullets of every child in school, whether the morsel interests him or not, even if it frightens him or sickens him, and even if there are other things that he is much more interested in learning. These ideas are absurd and harmful nonsense. We will not begin to have true education or real learning in our schools until we sweep this nonsense out of the way. Schools should be a place where children learn what they most want to know, instead of what we think they ought to know.
>
> (Holt, 1969: 171)

In 2000, students in Finland are being offered a new national strategy for the Information Society. In this most connected of countries, upper secondary education is to become an online activity. Those students who wish to will be able to opt to study from home or from open learning centres through distance education methods (http://www.oph.fi/etalaukio/english.html). Similarly, in the Netherlands, a pilot project during the upper secondary years in 1998–9 led to a full-scale move to a distance education option at the upper secondary level in the academic year 1999–2000.

In the UK, areas such as Birmingham and Clackmannanshire are experimenting with other models. Researchers are proposing ways forward, and teachers, as ever, are choosing what works, rejecting the unproven and coping with change in the way that has become second nature to so many of them. It is to the teacher that we must turn to see the face of online education, not to the software developer or computer manufacturer. It is the teacher that will be the key to learning in the future, just as it has been the teacher that has been the focal point in the past. Teaching will change and schools may well be transformed into something quite different from their present manifestation, especially in the upper secondary years. A teacher at the beginning of the twenty-first century will need many of the same skills needed a hundred years ago, but to these should be added the adaptability, flexibility and understanding needed to function in the ICT-supported learning arena. School buildings are beginning to look threatened; the local primary school may have a secure future as a community learning centre, but the large secondary school is increasingly difficult to justify as more countries start developing models for older students based on open and flexible learning in neighbourhood sites. At a time of such rapid and sometimes bewildering change it is reassuring to conclude that the teacher–student relationship is so central to the learning process that no technology can replace it. Whether it be as Peripatetic Electronic Teacher, as proposed by Squires, as the ICT trained and tested teacher insisted upon by the Teacher Training Agency in the UK, or some other manifestation not yet apparent, teachers look likely to be around for a while yet.

Chapter Summary

- National ICT policies often reflect national priorities and approaches in obvious and more subtle ways.
- Countries which seek to dominate and lead will see different ICT uses developing from those in which the emphasis is on communication and cooperation.
- Despite the differences, there are many common agendas across Europe regarding the development of appropriate uses of ICT in education.
- The European Union is becoming an extremely influential agent in educational ICT development and theorising.
- Changes in the geographical base of learning, the school or classroom, have been long predicted but now seem to be approaching.
- Much can be learnt from those local education authorities or teachers who have published their plans and experiences.
- A series of key initiatives related to alternative models of schooling in the upper secondary years will form the test-bed for change in the next two to five years.
- The changes caused by the arrival of ICT are irrevocable.
- Teachers will always be central to schooling – and learning.

Bibliography

Alspaugh, J. W. (1999). The relationship between the number of students per computer and educational outcomes. *Journal of Educational Computing Research*, 21 (2), 141–50.
Bayliss, V. (1999). *Redefining Schooling*. London: Royal Society of Arts.

Brighouse, T. (1999). A vision for our schools in the year 2020. *The Independent*, 5 October.

Committee of Ministers (1999). Declaration on a European Policy for new Information Technologies, 104th session, 7 May. Budapest: Council of Europe.

DfEE (1997). *Connecting the Learning Society*. London: HMSO.

Donnelly, J. (ed.). (1995). *IT in Schools: A Handbook for Senior Managers*. Birmingham: The Questions Publishing Company.

Grey, D. (1999). *The Internet in School*. London: Cassell.

Head, J. (1999). *Understanding the Boys: Issues of Behaviour and Achievement*. London: Falmer Press.

Holt, J. (1969). *How Children Fail*. Harmondsworth: Penguin.

Illich, I. (1973). *Deschooling Society*. Harmondsworth: Penguin.

Millard, E. (1997). *Differently Literate: Boys, Girls and the Schooling of Literacy*. London: Falmer Press.

Ministry for Education and Science, Sweden (ed.) (1998). *Tools for Learning IT: A National Programme for ICT in Schools*. Stockholm: Ministry for Education and Science, Sweden.

O'Sullivan, J. (2000). Traditional classrooms and teachers are out as cyber-school prepares to go online. *The Independent*, 21 March.

Passey, D. (ed.) (1998). *2000 and Beyond: A School Odyssey*. Swindon: The British Computer Society.

Postman, N. (1995). *The End of Education: Redefining the Value of School*. New York: Alfred A. Knopf.

Postman, N. and Weingartner, C. (1971). *Teaching as a Subversive Activity*. London: Penguin.

Scrimshaw, P. (ed.) (1997). *Preparing for the Information Age: Synoptic Report of the Education Departments' Superhighways Initiative*. London: DfEE, DENI, Scottish Office, Welsh Office.

Slevin, J. (2000). *The Internet and Society*. Cambridge: Polity Press.

Spender, D. (1995). *Nattering on the Net: Women, Power and Cyberspace*. Melbourne: Spinifex Press.

Squires, D. (1999). Peripatetic electronic teachers in higher education. *ALT-J Association for Learning Technology Journal*, 7 (3), 52–63.

Tiffin, J. and Rajasingham, L. (1995). *In Search of the Virtual Class: Education in an Information Society*. London: Routledge.

Virtual-Society (2000). *Virtual Society? Get Real! conference*, Brunel University. Available: http://www.brunel.ac.uk/research/virtsoc/events/GetReal.htm [28 February 2000].

Index